# MANAGING
# YOUR
# MOUTH

# MANAGING YOUR MOUTH

## An Owner's Manual for Your Most Important Business Asset

# Robert L. Genua

American Management Association

New York • Atlanta • Boston • Chicago • Kansas City • San Francisco • Washington, D.C.
Brussels • Toronto • Mexico City

This book is available at a special
discount when ordered in bulk quantities.
For information, contact Special Sales Department,
AMACOM, a division of American Management Association,
1601 Broadway, New York, NY 10019.

This publication is designed to provide accurate and
authoritative information in regard to the subject matter
covered. It is sold with the understanding that the
publisher is not engaged in rendering legal, accounting,
or other professional service. If legal advice or other
expert assistance is required, the services of a competent
professional person should be sought.

Library of Congress Cataloging-in-Publication Data

Genua, Robert L.
    Managing your mouth / Robert L. Genua.
        p.      cm.
    Includes index.
    ISBN 0-8144-7803-4
    1. Communication in personnel management.   2. Interpersonal
communication.   3. Confidential communications.   4. Gossip—
Management.   I. Title.
HF5549.5.C6G46   1992
658.4'52—dc20
                                                    92-1406
                                                       CIP

Printing number

        13  14  15  16  17  18  19  20

For Frances C. Genua

# CONTENTS

# Preface

# Why Manage Your Mouth?

As we approach the end of the twentieth century, the world abounds with new opportunities. A fast-changing business and social climate demands frequent and dramatic shifts in the work places and private lives of people. More than ever before, competence in the area of interpersonal skills is needed to meet the business, individual, and group demands that are thrust upon us.

Words and movements form the basis of communications between people. On the surface, they appear to be simple actions and reactions. On closer examination, however, they are found to consist of a complex pattern of behaviors that are based on attitudes, knowledge, personalities, tasks, settings, and many other variables.

On a practical level, we will examine the use of verbal

communication in business and personal relationships. Our point of reference is the hypothesis that if there is any one factor that causes a person to succeed or fail in a major life endeavor, it is his or her control over verbal communication.

The *how, when,* and *why* of what a person says is central to effective interpersonal relationships. The listener or receiver of the message passes judgment on the speaker. That judgment influences perceptions. Those perceptions play a critical role in determining one's success or failure in dealing with others.

In the pages that follow, we will show you how you can gain clearer insight into the many aspects of one-on-one communication and make them work in your favor.

# Chapter One
# The Spoken Word

## Personal Communications

What makes the world go around? Some say, "Love makes the world go around." Others say, "Money makes the world go around." Still others say, "Communication makes the world go around." We communicate in complex ways, and we use an incredible variety of equipment and services to do it. Information is sent and received in many forms. The products of the electronic revolution are highly visible. At work, computer and communications systems help us accomplish daily tasks. At play, we succumb to a wide variety of electronic gadgets. We amuse ourselves with radio, television, compact discs, records, cassettes, computers, satellite receivers, and dozens of other devices. Joe Consumer has many choices available to satisfy his entertainment needs. Mary Business Person speeds her work day by virtue of having instant access to numerous information sources. Practically every aspect of our daily lives is touched by communications. Communications influence not only the way we spend our time and money but also our ability to compete in the work place and maintain our standard of living.

Despite all the exotic communications systems available, however, people still need to communicate with one another on a personal basis. We send memos, letters, and cards. We make chicken scratches on the margins of documents. Some of us write in the sky with smoke, or tow signs behind airplanes. We write love letters in the sand and graffiti on walls. We carve "I love you" on school desks. We speak to each other constantly in person and over the phone. Personal communication plays an important role in our lives.

Having thrived despite the sophisticated, hi-tech communications systems, personal communication will last for a long time to come. At present it remains our most widely used vehicle for communicating with one another. People still talk to each other. They love to talk to each other. They want to talk. They need to talk. They have to talk. It's part of human nature. Person-to-person communication is still king, and the spoken word is the jewel in the crown.

## The Spoken Word

Daily interactions involving people revolve around conversation. Because dialogue forms the basis for all human interaction, one's ability to converse intelligently is extremely important. Moreover, our effectiveness is a result of how we present ourselves to others, as well as how we are perceived.

As simple as conversing may seem on the surface, there are many complexities involved. It's not just plain old talking: It is delivering a message effectively. It is selling an idea. It is giving and receiving information. It is confiding, it is dismissing. Thus every time you open your mouth to speak you accept a challenge or run the risk of creating a problem for yourself. However, there is no alternative. You are stuck with the fact that you must speak to others. People have to speak to each other. Some have been doing a good job at it and others a poor job. The ones doing a good job are usually those that are getting further ahead in life.

## You Are What You Say

In New York City, people are fond of saying, "You are what you eat." Too much food and too little exercise and before you realize it, you're obese. You go around with a spare tire around your middle and your physical appearance suffers. On the other hand, if you eat the right foods, and exercise regularly, you look trim and attractive. Your outward appearance reflects your diet and exercise regimen.

In Southern California, people say, "You are what you drive." Being trim, tan, and good-looking is not enough. In addition, you must drive an automobile that makes a statement about you. The statement must reveal who you are, or at least who you think you are. If you drive an American car, such as a Chevy, a Dodge, or a Plymouth, forget it! You're not with the program! Obviously a nobody! However, if you drive a California Volkswagen (a Mercedes), a Porsche, a Jaguar, or a Rolls Royce convertible, then you are definitely with it.

In France there are different standards. "You are what you wear." Strolling down the Champs Élysées in Paris, on a nice July evening, or dining at Fouĝuet's, you are likely to be judged by the clothes on your back as well as your fashion accessories.

Around the world, whether you find yourself in New York, California, or Paris, different criteria exist in people's minds for judging other people. There is, however, a common denominator that everyone is judged by. The standard that is common to all cultures is the way people speak. As soon as people talk, regardless of what they eat, wear, or drive, they project inner selves and the façade fades. What they say, and the way they say it, peels away layers of veneer to reveal the real people underneath.

## A . . . Ten . . . Hut!

The perfect individual always says the right thing at the right time. The rest of us seem to say the wrong thing at the wrong time. This can be embarrassing. A friend of mine, who said the wrong thing at the wrong time once too often, finally made up a sign that read, "Do not engage mouth until brain is connected." He tacked it up on his wall as a constant reminder to help him think through his words before uttering them. And that's what it's all about. If you can't control the words that come out of your mouth, you are likely to say something wrong.

In the U.S. Army, the first thing you learn in basic training is how to "pop to" and stand at attention. The second thing you learn is how to manage your mouth. Millions of GIs have been told to "keep your bowels open and your mouth shut." It's that simple. If you follow that advice you will be successful in the army. If you don't, you will find yourself in big trouble.

Too bad that approach doesn't work in civilian life, where we would go down the tubes if we had to keep our mouths shut. We need to communicate. In fact, we talk so much, that we have developed a whole vocabulary to define just that—the spoken word. The following is but a fraction of the more popular words and phrases that we use to describe the way we talk:

If you talk too long, you're a windbag or a blabbermouth, you have diarrhea of the mouth, or you're verbose, or you're running off at the mouth.

If you defend yourself, you're talking back or spouting off or being snappy or defensive.

If you tell a tale out of school, you're a bigmouth or a tongue wagger, a loose lip or a gossip.

If you talk persuasively, you have a silver tongue or you're a smoothie or you're tricky.

If you tell a tall tale, you're a bull-thrower, full of malarkey or baloney, a storyteller or a crackpot.

If you tell a lie, you're a fibber or a liar.

If you tell a joke, you're a gas, a riot, a comedian, or a panic.

If you complain, you're bitchy, cranky, whining, moaning, groaning, or grousing.

If you make a wisecrack, you're a wiseguy, a smart aleck, a hotshot, punk, upstart, or crud.

If you tell it straight, you're corny, square, a nerd, or a jerk.

If you say it cool, you're jivy, hep, groovy, awesome, or with the program.

If you tell it poetically, you're a romantic.

If you rap it out, you're cool.

Say it fast, and you're a motormouth or you're hyper; say it slow, and you're a drag.

Stretch it out, and you're tedious; shorten it up, and you're curt.

Say it smoothly, and you're glib; use vulgarity, and you're crude.

Laugh, and you're a scream; titter, and you're hysterical; stammer, and you're nervous.

Tell it like it's not, and you're talking through your hat.

Tell it like it is, and you're okay.

Whether you mutter, moan, groan, shriek, whine, or yell, everything that comes out of your mouth is up for grabs. It will be heard and *interpreted* by others. And that interpretation—be it a plus or a minus—reflects on you. If it helps, it's a positive, a plus. If it harms us in any way, it's a negative, a minus.

An example of the power of the positive use of oral skills can be found by looking at the great orators and successful political leaders throughout history. They used their oral skills to capture and hold the attention of their constituents. This allowed them to exert the necessary influence and control to forward their purpose and achieve their objectives. Similarly, great artists and performers spend years fine tuning their verbal faculties. With the twist of a phrase they can warm up an audience—entertain, delight, amuse, and hold them spellbound. By tapping into the full potential of the spoken word, they reap rewards. They prove that there is power to be gained by making full use of the positive side of oral skills.

But forget the great artists and performers. What about you? How do you come across to others? How do others perceive you?

## Three Dimensions

At one time, the pen was considered "mightier than the sword." Now it is the mouth that is mightier than the sword. The spoken word has tremendous power over our daily lives. It is a force to be understood and reckoned with.

The transactions that occur during a verbal exchange are complex and varied. They have three dimensions: talking, thinking, and listening. During the course of a conversation, people talk, think, and listen on many levels, all of which involve many factors. Underneath words lie nuances and shades of meaning—undercurrents, overtones, and a host of other modifiers that color or alter the message of the spoken words.

The astute communicator, always a good listener, is aware of these subtleties. He or she can quickly determine where the other person is coming from and can read between the lines. Recognizing the many levels that people communicate on, these individuals are able to analyze what is said, and perhaps even more important, what is left unsaid, what hidden agendas exist, how information is being used, abused, or misdirected, and how much control the sender is attempting to exercise in the conversation.

While possessing the ability to understand what a conversation is really about is critical to having the outcome work in your favor, the other side of the coin is that others are trying to figure out where you are coming from at the same time! If you wish to gain the upper hand, then you must be able to outthink the other. A truly sharp communicator has mastery over the many variables involved in the process.

The key to mastering the process is complete control of

your own mouth. To achieve that level of control, you must understand the concepts and techniques that are involved. If you can improve the chances of success and influence the outcome of verbal exchanges in your favor, wouldn't it be worth some of your time and a little effort? Wouldn't it be nice to exercise control and exert influence over the listener? All you have to do is be aware of the subtleties involved and apply a few proven techniques. The combination of your heightened awareness and the application of the techniques will prepare you to manage your mouth and hopefully outflank your opponent.

## The Goal

My goal is to help you achieve your goal. I want to show you how you can learn to refrain from uttering one word or saying one sentence that you will later regret.

Being respected is a mark of success. We will show you some of the reasons that one person is held in high esteem and another is not. Why good verbal skills constitute a basis for power. How people gain prestige and maintain it. How being alert to common traps and pitfalls can keep you from being tripped. How to deal with the common problems that undermine effective verbal communication. We will provide tips and techniques that will help you not only to control the words that come out of your mouth, but to gain better insight into and understanding of where others are coming from, so that you can react appropriately. More specifically, you will be guided in the following areas:

- Mastering the art of saying the right thing at the right time
- Learning to appreciate the value of remaining silent and keeping things to yourself
- Developing skills to gain better control of verbal exchanges
- Handling situations in which it is important to contain information and protect it from spreading
- Knowing what to say and what not to say during a job interview
- Understanding personality problems and how they influence behavior
- Exploring gossip and its effect on human relations
- Dealing with sensitive and proprietary information
- Learning ways to obtain information and to refrain from divulging it
- Recognizing the pitfalls that exist in management situations such as meetings, and how to be on guard against them
- Understanding the role of nonverbals in interpreting meanings
- Acquiring other skills that can be brought to bear to help you manage your mouth more effectively for success

These topics provide the framework that will guide you in developing your ability to "manage your mouth for success." In the chapters that follow we will explore them in detail.

# Chapter Two
# A Management Skill

A modern manager must be effective. The management process involves planning, organizing, directing, coordinating, and controlling. And the individual manager, charged with making the process work, must have many skills at his command.

Business has long recognized the need for management skills, so much so that companies spend big dollars to develop skills in their managers by putting them through management development and training programs.

Sales training, product knowledge, negotiating, listening, motivating, supervising, leadership, and problem solving—these are but a few of the subject areas of management training brochures that flood today's business mail. One management skill, however, that is frequently overlooked—essential for success in business, essential for earning the respect of both subordinates and superiors—is the management of *what you say.*

It is generally recognized that people speak mainly from experience. The impact that our words have on others is significant, yet for the most part we tend to leave the outcome to chance.

This begs several questions. If the misuse of speech impacts our effectiveness in a negative manner, then isn't it incumbent upon us to strengthen our communications skills? Doesn't better communication deserve to be high on the list of our training and development priorities? Wouldn't it be a big plus to ourselves and our organizations, and even to our friends and families, if we could improve our skills in this area? And from a more selfish viewpoint, wouldn't it help us move ahead of the crowd?

## A Framework for Assessment

Verbal skills shape and support every interpersonal relationship. They represent a vital resource for developing one's competence as a professional, one's credibility as a communicator. To develop your skills in communication, you must first assess your strengths and weaknesses. This will aid you in understanding what you need to do to improve your skills.

A simple assessment tool, which can be applied to give you some insight into where your individual strengths and weaknesses lie, is a set of questions you can use to test yourself. Look at the following statements, and rate yourself on a scale of 1 to 4, based on how well each statement describes the way *you* engage in verbal interaction.

1 = not very characteristic
2 = somewhat characteristic
3 = generally characteristic
4 = very characteristic

1. I am a good listener. I am always attentive and receptive during verbal interaction.

2. When I first meet someone I try to make a good impression by relying more on what I say than on my physical appearance.

3. When I speak, my timing and delivery are good and have a noticeable effect on others.

4. I am animated when I speak, and my body language keeps the dialogue rolling.

5. I use volume and modulation in a conscious effort to reinforce the effect of what I say.

6. I always try to be friendly and outgoing with others when I engage in conversation. I want to be a friend rather than an enemy.

7. My interpersonal skills are the key to my success to date. They are my most important asset.

8. I understand the importance of self-control and I exercise it all the time.

9. I interact well with people because I fully understand all the elements that are involved.

10. I am always mindful of what I say, because I know the walls have ears.

11. I very rarely talk about or reveal sensitive information.

12. I can purposely remain silent because I have excellent control over every word that I speak.

13. I exercise control over what I say, even after I have had a few drinks.

14. I always feel compelled to confess or tell everything just to get it off my chest and clear the air.

15. I place very little trust in others.

16. I can keep a secret, so I don't have to worry about leaking information.

17. I feel that information leaks in a company are serious business and can have damaging repercussions.

18. I very rarely feel compelled to spill the beans; hence I know that I can keep a confidence.

19. I frequently deliver hidden clues in my conversation so that the astute listener can read between the lines and tune in my underlying messages.

20. I don't worry about arguments because I never get into them.

21. Self-control over what I say comes naturally to me.

22. I feel that I comport myself very well in most situations involving verbal interaction.

23. I exercise good control over my emotions when I am set up or baited. I can restrain myself from reacting in a manner that I will regret later on.

24. I understand my inner feelings, and I know why I say certain things.

25. I know when it is appropriate to speak and when I would be better off remaining silent.

26. I find it very difficult to keep sensitive information to myself, because I am not a secretive person.

27. I very rarely curse, because it is not appropriate to a business or social setting.

28. I am a good listener, yet I frequently fail to hear many things that are said to me.

29. In conversations I am very effective at using silence.

30. I am very good at persuading people to see my point of view or getting them to do what I want them to do.

31. As much as I would like to be a straight arrow, I don't feel that I could survive in this dog-eat-dog world if I always told the truth. So once in a while I lie.

How did you do? Total your points. If you scored 80 points or above, you most likely do a good job at managing your mouth. You have a good understanding of and appreciation for the realities and sophistication of verbal exchange in the business world. You no doubt minimize your risks by employing a sound methodology that allows you to manage your mouth to your best advantage.

If you scored below 80, you need to gain a better understanding of the subtleties of good communication. Toward that end, let's review each statement and discuss the reasons why one approach may be more advantageous than other alternatives for achieving positive results—results that will work in *your* favor.

### 1. I am a good listener. I am always attentive and receptive during verbal interaction.

Whenever we talk, we take a risk—the risk of divulging too much of ourselves, betraying a confidence, or having information misunderstood, perhaps passed on erroneously and ending up used against us.

While an intelligent conversation requires both listening and responding, the good listener is more likely to have a subtle advantage.

The diagram below illustrates the cycle of interaction as it relates to high and low levels of risk. Follow the diagram around clockwise, beginning with the area of greatest liability at upper right. Note the degree of interaction and its relatively high degree of risk. Note that the odds of creating problems for yourself increase or decrease as a direct function of the amount of talking you do combined with your level of involvement.

I said above that the good listener is more likely to have an advantage. Why? Because—if you can envision a playground seesaw—the lower your risk, the higher the risk of the other party involved. As a result, you stand a better chance of learning more and revealing less, resulting in your gain, your opponent's loss.

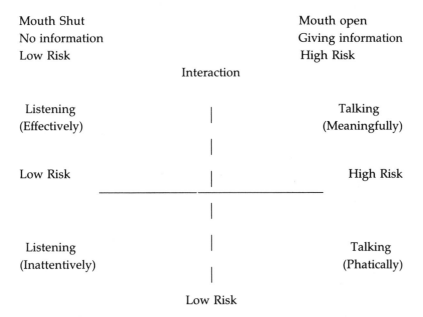

| Mouth Shut | | Mouth open |
| No information | | Giving information |
| Low Risk | | High Risk |
| | Interaction | |

| Listening | | Talking |
| (Effectively) | | (Meaningfully) |

| Low Risk | | High Risk |

| Listening | | Talking |
| (Inattentively) | | (Phatically) |

Low Risk

All you need to do is learn to control your talking (manage your mouth) and, at the same time, listen more effectively, and you will minimize your risk and at the same time maximize the risk of your opponent.

**2. When I first meet someone I try to make a good impression by relying more on what I say than on my physical appearance.**

First impressions are usually fairly accurate, and as such, they are hard to live down. But second impressions tend to be even more careful judgments, than first impressions, and as a result they can live on forever. As you interact on a continuing basis with your colleagues and acquaintances, you will be keenly judged. They will look past first impressions, sweep away your facade, and reach into the innermost depths of your intellect and personality. They will turn you inside out and X-ray you. As they interpret your words, they will assess your credibility. The words that you speak will carry the bulk of the burden of how you are perceived. By what you say, you will be known, and your actions will be relegated to a secondary role. The spoken word will make or break you.

**3. When I speak, my timing and delivery are good and have a noticeable effect on others.**

The spoken word has two close companions: timing and delivery. Words can sound dull and monotonous, or animated and exciting. How often have you heard a mundane topic brought to life by an enthusiastic speaker? or a great story put to sleep by poor delivery?

**4. I am animated when I speak, and my body language keeps the dialogue rolling.**

Body language consists of obvious and subtle, conscious and unconscious, body movements and facial expressions. And your body language provides additional clues that support (or belie!) the information you are verbally transmitting. Stepping in a little closer to the person you're addressing, looking directly at him or her, smiling, or myriad other movements, gestures, or expressions can either encourage conversation by putting the listener at ease, or discourage conversation by making him or her uncomfortable.

Some body and facial movements work to your benefit, others to your detriment. (Julius Fast is the guru of body language, and I recommend that you read his books on the subject if you are interested in pursuing it further.) Body language is a part of managing your mouth from the standpoint that it adds meaning to the words you speak. Augmenting your speech by body gestures, facial expressions, and movements will enliven your delivery and the better chance you will have of getting your intended message across. Enhancing the whole context of your discourse style makes it easier for the listener to receive your message.

It is also possible to communicate with another person without using words. Nonverbals, or body language, can carry as much weight as words, and sometimes even more. Nonverbals involve body movement such as the use of arms, legs, and the head. The term also covers the amount of eye contact that is made and how we position ourselves relative to one another. The movement of our body, along with the use of the spoken word, gets the full meaning across to the listener.

Body language is so powerful that sometimes you can't hide the truth with words. It's a fact—your body doesn't know how to lie. Every movement that you make sends a message, and that message either reinforces or contradicts your words. The truth prevails. People's words can be figuratively shrouded in an atmosphere of fog and torrential rain. They can be clouded by diatribe and highly animated body language. As a result, the actual words are only a part of the total message that the listener receives.

Parallel to the spoken word is a silent language that consists of all of the additional signals that the listener responds to in the course of the conversation.

There is a disease called aphasia, which results from a brain lesion that leaves its victims with extreme difficulty or total loss of the ability to use words. However, aphasics remain extremely sensitive to body language. They compensate for this impairment with the capacity to pick up on slight nuances in facial expression, changes in inflection, tone, and timing. Friends, relatives, and people that take care of aphasics attest to the fact that it is virtually impossible to lie to them. Aphasics cannot grasp the meaning of words. As a result, they are not deceived by words themselves. They are able, however, to grasp precisely the meaning of a verbal exchange. That message is derived from the body language that the sender transmits. Even though aphasics cannot understand the spoken word, they can interpret the nonverbals—the smiles, frowns, grimaces, false gestures, false tones, and other signals that transmit the truth behind the words.

### 5. I use volume and modulation in a conscious effort to reinforce the effect of what I say.

The use of volume and modulation can alter the meaning of the words and lead to a different interpretation. Properly applied, it can help you to project zest and enthusiasm instead of boredom and disinterest.

A case in point is the way that a simple rise in tone at the end of a sentence can make a huge difference *in how one is perceived*. When George Bush was campaigning for President, he was frequently described as a "whiner." This perception resulted from the fact that Mr. Bush raised the tone of the last word in each sentence, ending with a word that was a pitch or two higher than the rest.

On the other hand, if the last word in a sentence is dropped a pitch or two, the sentence sounds full of power and authority. The movie actor John Wayne mastered that nuance and projected a commanding presence to his audience. Mr. Bush learned the secret of avoiding the rise in pitch in the last word of a sentence, and the result was dramatic. I believe that changing his delivery was a strong contributing factor to his more positive image. Volume, modulation, pitch, and every nuance of human speech are extremely important. They can project inner strength, support or backing instead of weakness, criticism or detraction. The complexities of verbal communication between humans separates those exchanges from all other forms of interaction. They are distinctly human and they are distinctly personal. They embrace a wide range of emotional, physical, and mental processes that provide the backdrop for the spoken word.

6. **I always try to be friendly and outgoing with others when I engage in conversation. I want to be a friend rather than an enemy.**

Each verbal exchange between people is a two-way street. That street can either build a bond between people or it can drive a wedge between them.

When people build bonds they tend to provide each other with similar responses—they are usually agreeable, friendly, and helpful, and they establish an easy, comfortable relationship. On the other hand, when individuals are in conflict with each other they use words and body language that set them 180 degrees apart. This polarization occurs as a result of large differences in verbal style as well as intent.

In some cases this isn't all bad, because opposing viewpoints are often helpful in arriving at sound decisions. What is less than desirable, however, is that long after the decision has been made the behavior that preceded it is remembered. This results in the battle being won but the long-term relationship being destroyed. In practice, it is easy to get drawn into a discussion where long-term interpersonal relationships are at stake. One person reflects on being drawn into such a situation, which caused irreparable harm to both her and her career.

> During the meeting, a point came up with regard to customer service. I took issue with the

way that a customer's complaint was to be handled. The proponent of the idea insisted that there was only one way to handle the complaint. She proposed that the only time we would rectify the customer's complaint was when the customer squawked loud and clear. I don't even remember what the nature of the complaint was. All I remember is that I felt that it was not an honest way to conduct business.

I could not restrain myself, and I attacked her on the basis of her lack of integrity and her dishonesty. Even though I felt at the time, and still feel, that I was on solid ground, I regret the fact that I attacked her personally. I not only incurred her ill feelings, but I managed to alienate and turn off everyone in the group.

That was over two years ago and I still am suffering the consequences. As I said earlier, I don't even remember what the subject was, but I and everyone else in the meeting—to this day—remembers my behavior.

7. **My interpersonal skills are the key to my success to date. They are my most important asset.**

Good interpersonal skills are vital for success in any endeavor that requires contact with other humans. They are a valuable asset that is not easy to come by. Superior interpersonal skills are the end product of experience, education, and training. They are driven by thoughts, feelings, sensitivities, and subjective biases.

The interaction of all those variables are at the heart of every relationship. Success or failure depends on how skilled one is in their use. Good skills will help you succeed; poor skills will doom you to failure. Good skills will make friends; poor skills will lose them.

### 8. I understand the importance of self-control and I exercise it all the time.

Control is the toughest part of managing one's mouth. Words must be monitored, and *you* must monitor them. In addition, you must make sure that your words serve your best interests.

Your effectiveness depends not only on what you say and how you say it, but also on how another person perceives you. Your choice of words, your inflection, your timing, tone, mannerisms, and body language together shape your intended meaning and influence the perception of the listener.

The process of managing one's mouth takes place at many levels and in many diverse situations. There is a right way to utilize the gift of the spoken word, and there are many ways to abuse it.

Talking and listening between individuals, in one-on-one situations or in group meetings, in both formal and informal contexts, is loaded with traps. (An exploration of the pitfalls and consequences of using your tongue indiscriminately will underscore the hazards.) The degree to which you practice control in verbal interaction can mean the difference between success and failure. Your success depends on how well you utilize your intelligence and—perhaps even more important—your *judgment.*

### 9. I interact well with people because I fully understand all the elements that are involved.

Interaction between humans consists of many variables. It involves personality, intelligence, interpersonal skills, and many innate characteristics of the participants. Before a single word is spoken, the elements of interaction begin to work. Those elements shape the output, which is the spoken word. Key to this interaction is intellect and judgment. To gain better control over what you say, you must be able to combine your intellectual ability with judgment.

Intellectual ability is the power that you have to think clearly and incisively about specific facts and also about abstractions. Judgment, on the other hand, consists of your ability to combine conclusions with social awareness so that they are acceptable to the people that will be affected by them. If you cannot combine your intellectual ability with judgment, you do not have control—regardless of how smart you are. It makes no sense whatsoever to be "brilliant" if you are unwilling or unable to adjust your conclusion to fit the situation. You may be right as rain, but you will be standing out in left field if your judgment does not mesh with the situation. Invariably your conclusion will be rejected by the people that are affected by it.

A step-by-step process for developing your ability to gain better control over what you say is as follows. Let's assume for the moment that you want to gain control over a situation that involves dealing with information that has been making the rounds and has everyone excited.

First, write it down on a piece of paper. Ask yourself, what seems to be the main point that this information contains and what seem to be supporting points? Write them down. Ask yourself, what information do I have here that is actual fact and what information appears to be errors, or omissions. Ask yourself, what is it about this information that has people stirred up and why is it making the rounds on the grapevine? Add to your notes the role of the person or persons that the information affects firsthand. Write down what you think his or her problems will be as a result of it.

Now, organize the factual information. Address questions directly to the individual that passed the information on to you. Do not talk to anyone else about it. The questioning at first should be directed toward finding out about the what, when, where, why, and how of the information and the situation in which it came into the individual's possession. Try to pin down the source. Who did he or she hear it from? Who was there? Who else heard it? What else was said at the time? Try to elicit as much information as you can from your source. Clues should be tracked down if they offer any insight as to why the information is being spread around.

Then, formulate an issue. After you have gathered the information, ask yourself, what is at stake here? Is it an organization problem or a personal problem? What are the potential problems that this information can cause? What can happen to the people that are immediately concerned? Is it a problem that deserves management attention and/or direct involvement?

Now, crystallize your decision. Write down how you will handle the information from this point on. What will you do with it? Here are the options:

- Say nothing and keep it to yourself.
- Contact the principals involved and tell them what you heard.
- Tell only your closest friend, a relative, or your spouse.
- Embellish the information and pass it on.

And finally, weighing your course of action, write down the pros and cons for the choice you made. Analyze your decision and try to learn from the exercise as a whole. After you have had a chance to study your reaction to this exercise, review the whole exercise and reflect on it. What was the sequence of events and what behavior accompanied them? What information was passed on that may create difficulties for individuals and/or the organization? How, if at all, might the spread of the information have been prevented and what, if any, truth was contained in it?

Ask yourself, what would my role have been in this instance? Would I join in and participate in the passing of the information? And to what extent? And now that I am reading this book, would my behavior be any different?

Am I gaining any insight into this problem? Am I learning how to "manage my mouth"? Do I realize that, like any other skill, this is something I will have to work on. And that I will have to unlearn my old habits and train myself in the new ones? I will need insight into my strengths and weaknesses and the resolve to see it through. That is, if I want to be any good at managing my mouth.

**10. I am always mindful of what I say, because I know the walls have ears.**

Be careful, you never know who is listening. Whether you're in an elevator, the lavatory, an airplane, or a cab, the walls have ears. I have "overheard" many private conversations and, I may add, unintentionally, not by eavesdropping. I'm talking about insensitive people speaking in loud voices. People discussing sensitive subjects in public. People who seem totally unconcerned over who hears them.

**11. I very rarely talk about or reveal sensitive information.**

A grade-school joke used to be told about the three fastest ways to spread the news. They were telegraph, telephone, or telefriend. Sensitive information is easily compromised. In developing your ability to manage your mouth you should think twice, whenever you get on the phone or otherwise communicate with anyone, as to where the conversation may take you. It is so very, very easy to fall into the trap of talking too much. Let's face it. It is a highly civilized, social thing to do. And you want to be as friendly and sociable as the next person. Yet, you must restrict what you say. You must practice restraint so that you do not compromise yourself.

## 12. I can purposely remain silent because I have excellent control over every word that I speak.

Knowing when to say something and when to leave certain things unsaid is half the battle. How many times have you said something that you wished you could retract? Oh, you thought, if only I could have kept my mouth shut. Too late! It got out and everyone heard it. Here is a story that made the rounds.

A top-level executive was delivering a speech at a management meeting of over three hundred people in the posh ballroom of an exclusive hotel. While he was standing at the lectern and speaking, a peer of his made a sarcastic remark from the audience. Rather than respond to the remark in kind, he gracefully looked up at the ceiling and said, "Oh, Lord, please keep me from saying what's on my mind."

That demonstration of control and poise resulted in a big round of applause from the audience. The speaker had clearly won them over. The individual who had interrupted the speech with his caustic remark glowed red from embarrassment.

Oftentimes you are much better off keeping your mouth shut than taking the bull by the horns and rising to the challenge of meeting one barb by throwing a barb of your own. It is somewhat akin to the philosophy of turning the other cheek. In the long run you will be better off if you carefully consider what you are about to say and decide that it is better left unsaid.

### 13. I exercise control over what I say, even after I have had a few drinks.

In wine there is truth, so be careful around booze. For several centuries that expression has proven itself to be absolutely right-on. After a few drinks, individuals will spill their guts and tell you their life stories. The things that people will say under the influence of alcohol are unbelievable. For some reason, which many believe to be a lowering of inhibitions, individuals will share their most private thoughts. You must double your guard whenever you drink. On the "morning after" you may find yourself dismayed over the amount of information that you revealed while under the influence. Without sounding like a preacher, and at the risk of moralizing, my advice to you is to limit your intake so that you maintain total control over your body as well as your mind.

### 14. I always feel compelled to confess or tell everything just to get it off my chest and clear the air.

Regardless of what happens, don't ever admit to it. Many an American who served in the armed forces is familiar with the expression "Discretion is the better part of valor." Over the years, that has come to mean that you can do pretty much what you want to do as long as you don't tell anyone about it and as long as no one finds out. In other words, be discreet and people will think you are a good person. This is a critical lesson in managing your mouth, because it points up the fact that poor behavior would more than likely go undetected provided that information about it was not made available. On the other hand, if a person is valorous but makes one tiny mistake that happens to get some publicity, then he or she is in deep trouble. The point is simple. Once the word gets out, it can do you in. So don't let the word get out!

## 15. I place very little trust in others.

Call it cynical, call it wary, call it anything you like, but anytime anyone asks you to trust them, look out. People will go to great lengths to get others to confide in them. "Trust me, it won't go any further, I promise. Maybe I can help you." How many times have you heard that line? Based on my experiences, I don't know a living soul I would trust. As the pirates of old said, dead men tell no tales. Obviously live men talk. As a result, my advice is do not trust anyone with sensitive information. Especially those that go out of their way to wheedle it out of you. These people are often the very ones that are likely to let you down.

## 16. I can keep a secret, so I don't have to worry about leaking information.

If you value your reputation, then protect it at all costs. Once you earn the reputation for having the ability to keep a secret, you will be a trusted member of the management team. On the other hand, if you get the reputation of spreading information or being loose with it, you will not be trusted. As time goes by, you will be cut out of the mainstream and you will be ineffective. The end result will be that you will either stagnate in your current position or you will be maneuvered around to less-important positions. You will find that your career has dead-ended and that you will not be sought out for input into important projects. The trend toward cutting you out will most likely be gradual and subtle. But, nevertheless, it will be real. You don't have to go around breaching confidences every day; all it takes is one or two happenings, and you will find that you are perceived as a high risk who cannot be trusted with information. Once you get that rep, your career will be severely impacted.

## 17. I feel that information leaks in a company are serious business and can have damaging repercussions.

Keep your eye on the bottom line: the cost to the organization can be devastating. True, in many cases leaking information results in superficial damage. Maybe someone will get his nose out of joint for a brief period, or someone may be embarrassed. On the other hand, some

leaks wreak havoc and may cause an organization to top-
ple or go belly-up. History is full of incidents in which
leaked information caused widespread damage. During
the celebrated Iran-Contra hearings in the summer of 1987,
the congressional panel accused the White House staff of
leaking information. The White House staff, referred to as
the "1600 Pennsylvania Avenue Group," in turn accused
the Congress of being a constant source of leaks to the
public. During the hearings, both parties accused each
other of a lax attitude toward safeguarding sensitive information. The whole attitude of mistrust turned out to be
one of the key reasons why the National Security Council,
a part of the White House staff, was accused of intent to
subvert the law and go around the Congress to carry out
covert operations.

## 18. I very rarely feel compelled to spill the beans; hence I know that I can keep a confidence.

No matter how hard you try to contain information
within yourself, there will surely come a time when you
will be compelled to tell others. Only the most self-
disciplined person can truly keep a secret. There is a tendency on the part of mere mortals to bare their innermost
secrets to someone at some time or some place. All that is
needed is the proper setting. This could be after a few
drinks, during the course of a heated debate or an argument, as barter in exchange for a favor, or as therapy to get
a close friend to help share the burden. Whatever the reason, it is difficult to keep a secret. This point will be ham-

mered at continually throughout this book. The intent here is to regularly apprise you of Mother Nature and how the deck is stacked against you. You are born with the tendency to divulge sensitive information about yourself and others. You can win only by fighting it tooth and nail.

### 19. I unconsciously deliver hidden clues in my conversation so that the astute listener can read between the lines and tune in my underlying messages.

People are not dumb. A casual remark, which on the surface does not seem to be important, can turn out to be the loose thread that the listener needed to pull together the entire story. Here is a case in point. At one of the nation's leading aerospace test centers, an aviation magazine writer attended a series of unclassified briefings. As he rotated through several departments, each department head gave a stand-up presentation and told the group what the function of his or her department was, what they were working on, and several examples of their efforts to date. At no time did the department heads discuss any highly classified projects that they were working on.

The department heads then took questions from the floor and answered them as best they could without (so they thought) revealing any of the classified information. The very next edition of the aerospace magazine carried a lengthy article on the development of a new rocket nozzle. At the time, the concept, theory, and design of the nozzle were classified "Top Secret." To make matters worse, the whole project was proprietary to a private aerospace corporation. The writer covered in detail all the technical aspects of the nozzle, right down to the type of material that was used in its construction. When the article appeared in print, the high military brass at the organization were stunned. Even more appalled was the top management of the aerospace company. All parties were totally dismayed and shocked. "How could such a leak have occurred?" they asked. To find out, they launched a full-scale investigation into the cause of the leak. It was a major breach of security, and it compromised a major piece of hardware that was being developed as a part of America's nuclear arsenal. Very serious business.

At the conclusion of the investigation, many changes in management were made and those responsible for the leak (and some that were not) were punished. The moral of the story is that any person who will spend the time to ferret out information can get the bits and pieces from unwitting sources. These suppliers of information are often innocent, unaware that they are providing the wherewithal for a spy or a fortune seeker or an honest journalist to come up with the full and complete details of the story.

How do you safeguard against this? Always look beyond the question and ask yourself what constitutes the motivation behind a line of questioning. Why is the person asking these questions and what is he or she trying to get at? As in the parlor game Twenty Questions, it generally takes twenty questions or so to piece together any story. So beware of any question that even comes close to a sensitive issue. To do otherwise may cause you to be an unwitting supplier of information, and to possibly end up the target of a "management change."

## 20. I don't worry about arguments because I never get into them.

Sooner or later during the course of your career you *will* be drawn into an argument. Arguments generally start over simple matters and have a nasty tendency to escalate into ugly scenes. No matter how gentle your disposition or how easygoing you are, at some time or another someone is going to tick you off and you will find yourself in a kicking and hollering mood as the argument heats up.

In these situations you are at your most vulnerable. If you are normal, you are apt to say anything. One word will lead to another and a barrage of words will spew out. More than likely many of them will be curse words and expletives.

The only method available to you to manage your mouth in a situation like this is to avoid getting into the situation in the first place. To do this you must recognize the early symptoms of an argument in the making. These are the early signs: the discussion starts to drift off the main subject and red herrings are brought in; the discussion begins to get subjective and departs from the objective; personalities start to enter the picture and name calling takes place; the tone, choice of words, and volume and speed of delivery start to escalate, and the remarks become sharper and more devastating; tempers start to flare, and it begins to feel as if someone is going to get punched out, as words are losing their impact and physical violence appears to be the only solution.

How do you handle this? You must back down. Only a

fool would persist. You must try to stop the argument from developing. The earlier that you recognize the symptoms, the better. Under no circumstances are you to allow the argument to develop to the point where someone has to lose face. The days of dueling are out, as well as the days of defending one's manhood or other such nonsense. They have no place in the business world.

If you care anything about your career, you must step back and settle the argument in a respectful and tactful manner. By this, I don't mean asking your opponent to "step outside." I mean that you must say something to the effect that "if you continue to discuss this subject in that tone of voice then I am afraid that the conversation is over." That's it! If the adversary continues to bait you, then you must ignore him or her. The same applies to your role when two others are starting to argue. If you are a good manager, then you must intercede and demand that the discussion get back on track. If necessary the meeting should be adjourned or the group dispersed until tempers are back under control.

If there is one lesson that must be learned, it is simply that long after an incident occurs wherein a heated argument takes place, the subject matter of the incident is usually forgotten. What is remembered however is the behavior that took place. I assure you that the incident will be grapevined throughout the organization and the behavior of the combatants will be embellished and magnified. In the extreme, it will become a "war story" in the annals of the organization. It will be related to for many years to come. The reputations of the participants will forever be tarnished by their behavior in an unguarded moment in their careers.

## 21. Self-control over what I say comes naturally to me.

For most people self-restraint does not come naturally. Unfortunately the opposite is true. Talking too much comes naturally. Controlling the talk is more unnatural, if anything. Most of the time it is forced. Effective management of one's mouth, like any other skill, requires practice. Unlike any other skill, it is the number one skill that can make or break you. Forget your education, experience, and personality; nothing happens until you say something. Everything hinges on what comes out of your mouth. All that you want out of life depends on it. If you don't have your act together, forget it, you will fail. If you're good at it, then you have woven the fabric that will make the rest—your entire personality, character, education, and experience—hang together. Is the president of your company smarter than everyone else? More than likely the answer is no. By the same token, how do you rate that person's ability to manage his or her mouth? Chances are he or she would rate very high in that department.

## 22. I feel that I comport myself very well in most situations involving verbal interaction.

How well you "handle" yourself translates into how well you communicate, how well you deal with information, how much or how little you say, and when and where you say it. That, in a nutshell, is why people are where they are. The people at the top got there because they know how to handle themselves in all kinds of situations.

Being able to manage your mouth is the most difficult skill to master. You have to overcome pitfalls such as emotion, experience, pride, expectations, pedantry, bravado, influence, position, and self-image. Emotion gets in the way when you react to something someone says. You want to fight back and defend your position. You want to show the other party up to be wrong. "I'm not going to sit here and take this crap! You're way off base! I'm going to take you down a peg! I'll show you who's who!"

Your experience works against you. You tell others that they're doing things all wrong. You tried to do it that way in the past and it didn't work. You try to tell them what needs to be done and how to go about doing it. They resent your mouth. Your bravado is a problem. You yell, "Lead, follow, or get out of the way!" or "Let me in, coach, I'm ready!"

Your colleagues wonder if you are for real. You're pedantic on occasion. You show off your knowledge. Mention any subject and you have all the answers. You have to get your two cents in on everything. Your pride is out of control. You want to show them a thing or two. You can't resist telling them, "Did it ever occur to you that I was the person really responsible for that stroke of genius in the first place?" Your ego runs amok. You tell your buddies, "Even if you don't want to know about it, let me tell you anyway. After all, I'm me and you should listen to what I have to say."

### 23. I do not react emotionally when I am set up or baited. I can restrain myself from reacting in a manner that I will regret later on.

It is human to respond instinctively to something if one is baited, provoked, or led into a situation that calls for a comment. It is precisely what the other person has tried to get you to do. You may find yourself set up or given a perfect opening within which you can get your two cents in. Before you do, stop and think what you are about to say. Bite your tongue, count to ten, tension bind, internalize it. No matter what tag is placed on it, refrain from saying something in the heat of the moment. By stopping or delaying your response you will invariably change your response. Your response will go from a "hip shot" response to a more carefully thought-out, responsible, calm, cool, and collected response.

As you can tell, various names have been applied to this technique. Because it works, a lot of people have hung different labels on it over time. They all boil down to one fundamental: Don't talk until you gather your wits. The more sophisticated terms, such as "internalizing" or "tension binding," are used to link the personal feelings that are aroused during verbal exchanges. Specifically, they describe the process whereby people can control themselves by recognizing what external stimuli are acting on them and setting up a safeguard to prevent them from reacting in a self-damaging manner—self-damaging in terms of their personal style, demeanor, and professionalism.

For example, you're in a situation and someone says to you, "Hell, just don't sit there. Say something. Aren't you going to contribute anything to this discussion, or are you going to sit there like a bump on a log?" If you rise to the bait and bite, you are going to say precisely the wrong thing at the wrong time. It is better to forgo the baiting, stick to remaining cool, and formulate your response. When you do respond, your response should contain a statement that pertains to the central issue that is on the table. Never let someone else provoke you.

Another example: You are in a meeting, and the group is discussing product pricing. Although the company has been achieving higher gross sales revenue, the unit volume has been down. In the past two quarters, all the gains in revenue have been by price increase, and the prices are now meeting with resistance in the marketplace. The sales force has voiced the concern that the products are perceived by the customers to be overpriced. The competition has been hammering away at that and has been taking sales away from your company. A solution to the problem was suggested by the national sales manager: offer large-volume discounts. This would, in effect, reduce the price to the largest customers, while retaining the price increases at the low-volume-user end.

You have been in the meeting quietly listening to the

pros and cons of offering large-volume discounts. You haven't said anything up to this point, as the problem is totally out of your sphere of influence. However, the national sales manager is not gaining any headway with this proposal, and the financial manager in charge of pricing is making a strong argument for retaining the integrity of the pricing policy, as it has driven the revenue to an all-time high. In frustration, the national sales manager turns to you. His main motive is to get the heat off himself for a moment by shifting the focus to someone else; the diversion will give him time to regain his composure and rethink his strategy for gaining approval of the discount policy. He turns to you and says, "Why don't we hear what Joe has to say? I'm sure he has the answer. He usually does when we get to these impasses." He has placed you on the spot, and the attention of the staff meeting is now focused on you.

Without so much as even hinting that you are angry at the national sales manager for putting you on the spot and for the cavalier method in which he has treated you, you instead address the specifics of the issue directly. You do not indulge in personalities or politics. You do not come out on one side at the expense of the other. You address your comments to the leader of the meeting, in this case the president, and you say, "Mr. President, I feel very strongly that the pricing policy that we have established over the past several years has been the correct one. I feel this way for three reasons. These are . . ." In the end, you win. End of story.

## 24. I understand my inner feelings, and I know why I say certain things.

Be truthful to yourself. If you're not, who else will be? Ask yourself why. What is motivating you? One of the hardest things for people to come to grips with is the reasons they say what they say. On many occasions I have wished that I could take back something I said. Alas, it was too late; they had already been spoken. In retrospect I asked myself, "Why did I say that in the first place?" The flippant answer that "it seemed like a good idea at the time" will undoubtedly work to your detriment.

A better answer is that we are not always in complete control of what we say or do and that our emotions are powerful motivators. Our tendency to blurt things out in response to stimuli is a very powerful human trait and one that is not readily understood or easily controlled.

## 25. I know when it is appropriate to speak and when I would be better off remaining silent.

The person who knows when to say something and when to shut up has the edge on the competition. It is very tempting to say something on every subject. It is a nice feeling to be somewhat pedantic and show off in front of your colleagues. It is also very gratifying at times to let others know that you are well informed and you know the scoop. The savvy manager, however, knows that there is a time and place for everything, and that control of the tongue is everything. If you show off once too often you may be branded as a know-it-all. If you let people know that you are in on everything that is going on, you can be branded as a busybody. The point is that you must control your tongue and be aware of the repercussions that can accrue if you speak out when you should remain silent.

"With age comes wisdom" is a saying that can be applied to the skills involved in the use of the spoken word. There is wisdom in the learned ability to manage one's mouth. Heightened sensitivity in human interaction is a skill that can be learned and developed. Its development can take time. You can learn by trial and error, hit and miss, or by conscious effort. Left to chance, it may take a lifetime to master. If you invest a little time and effort, the dividends can prove very rewarding. The fact that you are reading this book indicates that you are interested in increasing your awareness and understanding of this subject. The payoff will come when you begin to apply the concepts in your daily activities.

**26. I find it very difficult to keep sensitive information to myself, because I am not a secretive person.**

It is very difficult for an honest person to act secretively and get away with it. If you try to hide something, it usually shows. Uncharacteristic behavior will give you away; it will become apparent that you are trying to conceal something. Once someone knows that you are trying to hide something, he will try to extract it from you. Believe it or not, there is a technique that has been refined over the years to accomplish just that. Research has shown that by using an open-ended question followed by a pause, the secretive person will open up and spill the beans.

Here is how the first part of the technique is applied. There are two main types of questions: direct and indirect. The direct question can be answered with a simple "yes" or "no," e.g., "Do you think it will rain?" The indirect question is an open-ended one, one that makes you answer more completely, e.g., "What do you think the weather will be like today?"

The direct question can be answered adequately in a few words, whereas the open-ended question requires more than a few words for an adequate response. The open-ended question is purposely designed to allow you plenty of room in answering and to get you to open up and expand.

The second part of the technique—to use a pause to give the person answering enough time to do so—is always used along with the first. If the question is asked without the pause, the technique may fail. The skilled questioner will establish rapport with you by being friendly, ask you an open-ended question, and pause so that you will have to respond. The pause may be unbearably long, but the skilled questioner will usually wait it out until you respond.

By being aware of this technique you can circumvent it. Here is how. When the open-ended question is put to you, don't respond to it. Instead, ask for clarification. Say something like "What's that?" or "What do you want to know?" or "Can you be more specific?" Force the questioner to ask a direct question. Then you can answer it "yes," "no," or "maybe." In this manner you can avoid giving out any information. The best that your questioner can hope for will be a "yes." If you happen to answer "maybe" or "no," you will have retained your secret.

## 27. I very rarely curse, because it is not appropriate to a business or social setting.

Males believe that there are two sets of standards. They will use one set for mixed company and one set when they're with the boys. Most males feel uncomfortable when they use profane language around women. With the increasing number of women that are found in the workplace, the question of cursing has become a cause of irritation for both males and females. Men are irritated because they feel they always have to be on guard and carefully control their vocabulary. Women are concerned because they feel they are being treated differently from the males because of the perception, on the part of the males, that women are sensitive to foul language.

All languages have swear words, and all of us at one time or another have used them, in both mixed and unmixed company. Four-letter words used to be the sole province of males. Four-letter words were never heard on the air waves. Gradually, however, the restrictions have been lifted, and in the movies, on radio, and even on TV, foul language is almost commonplace. Swearing has become a part of everyday speech.

Some people go to great lengths to swear, even breaking up words into syllables so that they can insert a swear word in between! Despite widespread use, however, whenever a person curses there is a tendency among listeners to lower their opinion of that person. Indeed, the listener immediately forms an impression that portrays the user of the swear word as vulgar or, in today's vernacular, "a low-life."

Cursing can be roughly divided into three levels. These levels are mildly expletive words, socially unacceptable words, and immoral language. Mildly expletive words are words such as hell and damn. They are used quite often in everyday conversation, and most people are not offended by them. Both men and women will use them in mixed company. Socially unacceptable words are basically words that refer to bathroom or sexual activities. Society has set the ground rules for certain words that simply are not acceptable for public use. Immoral language is that which consists of words that violate rules set down by the church, e.g., violating the Bible's commandments and taking God's name in vain. Immoral language is usually offensive to both men and women alike.

In today's world, there is another dimension to cursing. It is the issue of sexual harassment. For example, if a man curses in mixed company and then turns to a woman in the group and says, "Please pardon my French," two considerations surface. First, the male feels that by saying this he is deferring to women in the group. Further, he believes that he is displaying his own set of ingrained manners and respect for females.

Second, the woman may feel that the male is discriminating against her. She has been singled out for special attention. That puts her on the spot, and she has to signal somehow that she accepts the male's request for pardon. She may have to acknowledge that acceptance with a nod or a similar gesture that says it's OK, I don't mind. On the other hand, suppose she does mind?

The solution for you, the reader, whether male or female, is to evaluate the effect cursing has on your personal communication style. Cursing cannot be justified, as it really has no positive effect on anyone. Just the opposite is true. It can have a negative effect on your image and can detract from your professionalism. Added to that is the possibility that you may offend someone. There is no reason to swear. There is an abundance of words in the dictionary that can be substituted for swear words. You do not have to risk your reputation by lowering yourself, and you don't have to resort to swearing to make yourself heard. My advice is to keep your language clean and your image intact. Pick and choose a few words to use as substitutes and you will be able to make your point just as effectively. The risk that you run in the company of the opposite sex will be minimized, your professional image will be better, and overall, you will be more effective in dealing with others.

### 28. I am a good listener, yet I frequently fail to hear many things that are said to me.

Listening is an important skill. While some people hear, others listen. There is a big difference. *Hearing* can be described as in one ear and out the other, while *listening* can be described as listening, processing the information, and understanding it. Even if you hear every word that is spoken, if you don't comprehend the meaning, very little, if any, value can be derived from it. On the other hand, when one listens and comprehends, then the full value of the message can be received.

Research shows that listening and comprehending are improved when the listener is focused on the speaker, when the words are reinforced by nonverbal clues, when the speaker stays on the subject and doesn't wander, when the listener interacts with the speaker by asking questions or nodding approval or disapproval, when judgment is suspended until the end, and when main points and supporting points are made clear.

Thus, when all those elements are present, there is a major difference between "listening" and "listening and comprehending." By understanding those elements, you will be able to control not only what you want the listener to hear but what you want the listener to understand or comprehend. That will also influence what you want the listener to retain and to recall at a later date.

Knowing why a good listener retains most of what he or she hears and why a poor listener does not can be applied as a tactic. Here is how the two skills are linked together.

A good listener prepares to listen and comprehend by going over in his mind everything that he knows about the subject under discussion. It could be the players involved, the tasks, prior record of progress made on the project, future plans of the company, costs, material, and so on.

As the listener anticipates what the speaker is about to say, the listener will look for similarities or differences between what he already knows and what will about to be heard. The listener will focus on the similarities and the differences, as well as on their respective advantages and disadvantages.

You as the speaker can exercise control over the listener being deliberately vague on key points of information. In addition, by limiting your elaboration or by restricting the number of examples that you give, you can greatly diminish the listener's ability to understand and retain whatever information you give out.

The burden of enabling a listener to understand what is being said lies on the shoulders of you the speaker. Along with that burden, however, is the opportunity to use that responsibility to your advantage. You can restrict the amount of information that you give out, and if you orchestrate it properly, you can create the illusion that you are being very open and free about the subject under discussion.

President Eisenhower, during his term of office, was very popular with the American people. He was also noted for his garbled syntax. On many occasions, he did not put his phrases together in an orderly or harmonious pattern but rather in a disconnected fashion, hence many people did not really comprehend what the President said or meant.

His pattern of speech, however, allowed him to skate around many subjects. Whether he did this intentionally or not is left to historians to ponder, but the result was that he always managed to address controversial subjects without infuriating his detractors. (Quite possibly due to the fact that they did *not* fully understand what he said!) He was very effective in controlling his innermost thoughts and plans until such time that he wanted to reveal them in their entirety. At that time, his "garbled syntax" disappeared, and he came through loud and clear!

A second critical dimension that a good listener must possess is the ability to summarize mentally what the speaker has said, to recognize the speaker's main points and the supporting points that are used to substantiate them. By doing this, a good listener will retain more of the information he has heard.

For example, if you were discussing with a colleague the fact that there was going to be a price increase in the product line, and you wanted the listener to understand and retain that, you might say, "The company will initiate a price increase on September 1. Along with the price increase there will be a companywide meeting, and new price lists will be distributed. Additionally, training in the new price list will commence two weeks prior to the effective date." The main point of this statement is that a price increase will take place September 1. The supporting points are the companywide meeting and the training. A good listener will remember the main point and the supporting points and will most likely retain that information for some time.

If, on the other hand, you do not want the listener to retain the information, you minimize the main point and make no supporting statements. You would be vague, saying, "I don't know if any price increases are in the wind," and let it go at that.

The final key to thwarting a good listener is to be able to put up blocks or obstacles that will keep the person from listening effectively. These blocks can be environmental factors such as sights and sounds that will distract his or her attention. You can bait the listener by throwing out personal opinions or statements that will arouse him or her to a highly emotional state, which will prevent the listener from getting the entire message. Sometimes the use of improper grammar or slang will force the attention of the listener to the structure of the sentence rather than to its content and meaning.

You should also be aware that even the best listeners will listen selectively. They will hear only what they want to hear and they will tune out everything else. Generally, listeners are more effective in the morning than they are after a long day. Hence, if you have to discuss any subject that you do not really want to be understood, the best time to do it is when the listener has been suffering from an information overload or cannot concentrate fully on the subject at hand. Right after lunch, in a noisy environment, is as good a choice as any.

**29. In conversations I am very effective at using silence.**

Silence is not always golden. Why, you may ask, is it necessary to try to foil the listener's ability to understand what you say? Wouldn't it be easier simply to remain silent and not speak out on the subject? Yes, in some cases it is true that the best course of action is silence.

Oftentimes, however, it is important that you respond to situations that call for you to make comments. Rather than simply trying to mutter through the situation, you must skillfully control what you say so that you do a minimal amount of damage. If, in this situation, you can get the feeling across that you say a lot but it is content-free, or if someone describes you as a person who likes to hear himself talk but doesn't really say anything, then you are learning the art of managing the exchange of thoughts and ideas!

**30. I am very good at persuading people to see my point of view or getting them to do what I want them to do.**

The ability to influence people to take action that you want them to take is a key skill. It used to go under the heading of "persuasion," but today it is commonly referred to as "selling." All too often, selling is described as something that one is gifted with at birth—an art rather than a skill. The perennial question "Are salespersons born or made?" is still argued today. Modern-day training and development professionals will tell you that selling is a skill. It can be taught, and it can be developed through training. That is nothing really new. Back in the days of Cicero's orations against Catiline in the Roman Forum, Cicero had developed an early form of selling or persuasion skills. First he would verbally describe his proposal, then he would recite all of the benefits that would accrue when his proposal was accepted. Then instead of waiting for any objections to be put forth, Cicero would raise objections to his own proposal. Then, persuasively, he would handle or overcome each objection, until his opponent could find little if any fault in the proposal. With all of the objections overcome, he would then "close" his argument by asking for the adoption of his proposal.

Down through the ages this process has not changed very much. The skills are basically the same. However, the names of the skills have changed. In today's business world, a professional sales call consists of opening the call by establishing rapport with the customer. This is accomplished by making a general benefit statement that ties into a possible need of the client's. Then the salesperson questions the client in order to further uncover and define the client's needs.

Throughout the sales call, the salesperson introduces benefits of his or her product and skillfully overcomes objections. Finally, after all the objections have been handled, the salesperson assumes the close, asks for the order, and treats the situation as if the client has already bought the product or service by calling the product "his" or "hers": "Your product will be delivered on Monday. Please sign this purchase order." If the client refuses to sign the purchase order, then the professional salesperson doesn't throw in the towel. Rather, he or she goes back and uncovers the reason(s) for the refusal to buy, until the objection is overcome. Then another close is attempted. If the sales rep handles the skills correctly, and satisfies the needs of the buyer, then a sale takes place. The persuasion skills of old, wrapped in new clothes, are alive and well in the twentieth century.

**31. As much as I would like to be a straight arrow, I don't feel that I could survive in this dog-eat-dog world if I always told the truth. So once in a while I lie.**

If withholding any portion of the whole truth is lying, then many people "lie," but most business people would understand this reticence. No one expects an individual who is constantly negotiating or trying to gain ground to give away his or her position any more than you would expect a card player to openly display a hand. In communicating, you must be aware of the soundless words that parallel the communication of spoken words. There is an extraordinarily detailed vocabulary that consists of facial expressions. When you add together all of the other animated activities that surround the spoken word, the truth or untruth of your statement can be either carefully concealed or flagrantly revealed.

A tactic that you must master in managing your mouth is that of ensuring that you send the correct message to the receiver if that is what you intend. If you are trying to conceal the truth, and you end up blushing, stammering, or showing intense nervousness, then surely you will not be believed by the listener. On the other hand, if you are perceived as a believable individual, then the chances are your credibility will be greatly increased, even though you have carefully manipulated the spoken words. Overall,

your goal must be to convince the listener of the truthful-
ness behind your statements, so that he or she will not be
suspicious of any underlying untruths. Let's not be naive.
If you want to tell the truth, all you have to do is blurt it
out. If, however, you are trying to shape or influence the
outcome of a situation, then you must carefully consider
your choice of words and the accompanying body language to establish and maintain the credibility necessary
for you to achieve your goals.

# Chapter Three

# Guiding Your Development Toward a Better-Managed Mouth

## Reaching Your Potential

Self-development is a learning experience that can be stimulating and rewarding. By investing some time and effort, you can acquire new skills, concepts, ideas, and techniques that will improve your performance. Developing yourself, however, is like pulling yourself up by your own bootstraps. It is very hard to do. Many ingredients have to be present for the learning to take place. Two of the most important are motivation and growth potential, or receptivity to change. Let's take a look at motivation.

A motivated learner is one who actively pursues a subject, and has a definite purpose in mind and a specific objective in sight. The fact that you are reading this book says something for your level of motivation. Your purpose is to improve the way you conduct yourself in verbal transactions. Your objective is to become more effective in business and personal relations. But how do you go about doing that? The answer is that you have to learn and, by so doing, grow. In order to grow you have to be receptive to change. You must have growth potential.

"But," you may ask, "exactly what is meant by growth potential?"

The following example should help explain.

A while back I asked a colleague for his definition of "growth potential." He said that growth potential was the ability to assume greater responsibility and exercise greater decision-making authority within a given organization structure.

I turned to another colleague and asked him the same question. His response was quite different. He said that growth potential was a personal characteristic that allowed a person to learn from his mistakes, adjust his behavior accordingly, thus to grow as a person and, in turn, as a manager and an executive.

I agree with the latter definition. Many times I have seen high-potential people fail because they lacked growth potential. Unable to learn from their mistakes, they would not accept constructive criticism, and they used their intelligence to defend themselves rather than to listen, learn, and grow. The following is a case in point.

A very bright, promising junior executive could not grasp the importance of having been told, on more than one occasion, that he lacked judgment. Instead of using his intelligence to accept and correct that deficiency, he resisted the idea and used every ounce of his brain power to argue in defense of his belief that his judgment ability was as good as anyone else's. After several more instances of exercising poor judgment, and repeated attempts on his part to defend his weakness rather than try to recognize his problem, he was forced to leave the company. In fact, he was fired. The reason given—poor judgment.

The numerous attempts by others to help the individual recognize his shortcoming, and work to overcome it, had failed. He had rejected their advice. He felt he knew it all and he persisted in his ways. The result was that he failed, and his failure purely and simply was due to his unwillingness and lack of receptivity to change. He lacked growth potential.

To be successful in your self-development efforts you must have growth potential. Once you gain a good foundation of the many concepts involved in managing your mouth, you must apply those concepts to your daily activities. As you do that, you must be willing to observe and listen to the reactions of others, to what others have to say about you, and to what your own insight tells you. You will have to carefully consider whatever criticism is directed against you and evaluate it objectively. Once you determine it has merit or value, then assimilate it and change. Your growth and development depends on it. Now that your mind-set is in the mood for self-development, let's get the process under way. We will start by examining the relationship between personality and behavior, both of which play an important role in managing your mouth.

## Behavior

Behavior has three basic aspects. These are feelings, thoughts, and overt actions.

Feelings dictate how a person will behave in a certain situation. Very often a person may be unaware of the nature of his or her feelings and their effect. Some individuals will deny their feelings or suppress them. Many British are thought to do this as a matter of routine—it is known as "keeping a stiff upper lip."

To be in control of your behavior, it is not only important but absolutely essential that you be sensitive to your feelings and recognize the effect they have on you.

Thoughts and ideas are generated from current knowledge, a specific situation, and the prior experiences one has had in similar types of situations. By analyzing these factors, ideas come to mind about the courses of action that can be taken. These, in turn, act to influence your behavior.

The need for overt action that develops out of a situation varies for each individual. Needs develop from internal forces that motivate or push individuals toward certain types of action.

For example, when confronted by higher authority, one may shrink from expressing an honest viewpoint for fear of losing a job. This fear may result in saying or doing nothing. In another situation, such as dealing with a subordinate, the same individual could be precipitous and experience a strong need to do something. That need could stem from being angry, having a hot temper, or reacting from emotion. After the action is taken, and proves to do more harm than good, the individual might cop out and dismiss it. A fashionable way to cop out is to say, "It seemed like a good idea at the time." That, however, doesn't get one off the hook; it merely results in pushing off the problem till a later date. If action is to be taken, then you must understand and control the internal forces of thoughts, feelings, and how they influence your overt action.

These three elements—feelings, thoughts, overt actions—come together to influence your behavior. Here is an example:

You're in a hot and heavy staff meeting. The boss is supporting a proposal that you thoroughly disagree with. Your thoughts and ideas tell you he is wrong. Your feelings are mixed. You are concerned and excited and at the same time you fear your boss. You could risk scorn and ridicule and the repercussions that can result from challenging authority. Your action tendency is to say nothing and go along with the proposal. Your behavior in the situation above, or any situation, will depend on which of the three elements exerts the strongest influence on you.

Will your ideas and your feelings overcome the action tendency, leading you to make a solid contribution to the effort? Or will your other feelings contribute to your overt action tendencies, resulting in your blowing it? Will your perfectly logical and sound idea die aborning or will you be able to get it out on the table?

The interplay of these three elements is critical to managing your mouth. Your thoughts and ideas about what is being said will be triggered by what the other person says, and in turn, his or her thoughts and feelings will be triggered by what you say.

The interaction of these elements creates a situation. The situation eventually comes to a conclusion and the result is either in your favor or against you. The give and take in any situation depends on how the participants react to the stimuli that are present. The person who can exercise positive control over expressing his thoughts and feelings invariably comes out on top. That control stems from one's personality, the underlying factor that determines the degree of control that one can exercise in response to the stimuli.

## Personality

Your personality is the sum of your background, education, and experience. It is the primary internal influence on your behavior. It would be a great world if everyone had a pleasant personality and got along well with everyone else. Such is not the case, and every one of us has a personality defect or two. Nobody is perfect. Everyone has a need to improve. If you reflect on your personal behavior and recognize the problems that result from a given behavior, the need becomes obvious. Once a personality problem is recognized and faced, steps can be taken to modify the undesirable behavior and improve responses. Personality problems are the root cause of many problems that arise in verbal transactions. A normal personality results in normal behavior, an abnormal personality in abnormal behavior.

If you are to improve yourself, you must be aware of the personality traits that trigger your words. Those traits form the basis for your behavior. They have been baked into your personality and are extremely difficult to change. In some cases, they are like stripes on a tiger, and you won't be able to change them. However, it is worth a try. At the very least, you should be aware of what they are, the way they work, and the role they play in the words you speak.

Positive personality traits work for success, while others work for failure. Personalities come in many shapes and sizes. The traits that cause problems are also the ones that have proven to be the most difficult to overcome. Some of these are:

- A lack of caution (in choice of words)
- Temperament or hotheadedness
- Stubbornness or pigheadedness
- Nervousness or the state of being continuously high-strung
- Submissiveness or wimpiness
- The tendency to be argumentative
- Self-righteousness or a holier-than-thou attitude
- A negative attitude
- Extreme competitiveness
- Dogmatism
- Egotism or self-centeredness

Your personality is the mechanism that feeds thoughts to your brain; your brain triggers the words that come out of your mouth. The words that come out of your mouth are part of your overt behavior, which is what other people see and hear. If you have a temper and are a hothead and you rant and rave when you are provoked or frustrated, then you must learn how to restrain yourself. Restraint could be as simple as counting to ten or biting your tongue.

Picture the following. You are engaged in a conversation, and the person that you are conversing with says something that irritates you. He or she gets you boiling mad. What do you do? Your first impulse may be to snap back with something you'll later regret. Instead, you take a deep breath, collect yourself, and "bite your tongue." Or if you are adverse to pain, you can slowly count to ten under your breath. If you can actually do this in a stressful situation, you will be well on your way to success in controlling your mouth when your temper flares.

Situations such as the one described above are very common in interpersonal communication. Control is the key to success. The subject of control has been carefully studied in management science. Some practitioners in the training and development area call it "tension binding," while others call it "internalizing." Regardless of the label placed on it, it boils down to the same thing—the ability to restrain oneself from saying something wrong in the heat of an argument. It is quite human to respond to something if one is baited, provoked, or led into a situation that calls for a comment. It may be that it is precisely what the other person has tried to get you to do. You may find yourself set up or given a perfect opening within which you can get your two cents in. Before you do, stop and think what you would like to say. How will it hang on the receiver? Will you have any regrets if you say it? Will you wish that you could retract the words and be sorry if you cannot?

The mere act of stopping or delaying your response will invariably change it. Your response will go from a "heat of the moment" type of response to a more thought-out, responsible, calm, cool, and collected response. Don't say anything at first. Keep your mouth shut. Collect your thoughts and then respond. The pause is vital. It provides the brain with a few seconds to think through the process. Those few seconds mean the difference between being in control and being out of control. They allow the brain to sift through the external stimuli that is acting on you and set up a safeguard to prevent the mouth from reacting ahead of time, usually in a manner that works against you. Hot words result in tarnishing your image. Stay calm. Don't let others bait and lure you into a trap. Stay above it by thinking through the situation, then giving a cool, calculated response that you can live with, and one that you will be respected for. As further aid to help you refrain from making dumb statements when you are angry, try venting your frustration by mentally telling off the other person. Then continue with your effort to maintain your threshold of tolerance.

Preachiness is a personality defect that is a little easier to deal with. Say, for example, you are so enthusiastic about a subject that you tend to preach. Preachers are called preachers because they express their ideas as facts. Further, they believe them to be doctrine or unassailable truth. Preachers are unwilling to evaluate other viewpoints and totally reject opposition to their ideas.

If you find yourself in the mode of a preacher, then stop and ask for opinions from others in the group. Present your ideas as topics for discussion. Ask others for their viewpoints. Finally, remember that people will respond better to you if you provide them with benefits rather than issue ultimatums. Also, if you are always trying to prove that others are wrong, and you are always right, you could be an egotist.

Egotism is a very difficult personality problem to deal with. The egotist is not satisfied with simply being right. He or she engages in a cruel attack on others to embarrass them or make them look bad in order to make themselves feel good. Eventually, this builds barriers between these individuals and their colleagues.

Once you recognize that your ego is a personality problem, then you are on your way to curing it. What's required is for you to work toward understanding the needs of others, putting up with their actions, and accepting the fact that their ideas may be every bit as good as yours, if not better.

An additional problem associated with egotism is that of bragging. The braggart is prone to passing out information freely. No one has to ask for it. The supplier has an ego and loves to let others know just how important he or she is. One of the common traps that people fall into is that of boasting or bragging about their accomplishments. The salesperson that just closed a big account lets all his buddies know about it during Friday night Happy Hour. The following Monday the competitors are at the client, trying to crash the account by offering a lower price.

The personality problem involving dogmatism is usually associated with youth. Sometimes a little knowledge can indeed be dangerous.

The person that is dogmatic is concerned only with truth, laws, and regulations. He or she goes by the book, knows what's right, knows what's wrong, and everything is black or white. There is no gray, and he or she will not listen to any other viewpoints.

This turns people off. If the dogmatic person is unwilling to listen, so are others. To correct this problem, the dogmatic person must become aware that people reject dogmatism. He or she must learn to be flexible in accepting and evaluating others' viewpoints and must look at situations objectively rather than at the doctrine they embrace. In time, most people grow out of this trait and realize that life contains many gray areas.

One of the worst personality disorders that affects the management of your mouth is the emotional reaction, closely related to temper and in direct response to stressful situations. Emotional reactions trigger words that interfere with your effectiveness. This can be controlled by realizing that no one is perfect and seeing to it that every time you make this mistake, you recognize it and work toward cutting down the number of occurrences in the future. When the emotion wells up in you, try to describe it in your mind so that you can understand what is happening to you. After that is done, take time to cool off before responding verbally.

Another difficult personality trait to overcome is that of submissiveness. Being submissive means one has the tendency to give in. The result is ineffectiveness. Submissive people tend to procrastinate. They also tend to straddle fences. They themselves never know on which side of the fence they will end up. It depends on which way the wind is blowing at the time. It has nothing to do with their own values or beliefs.

You can improve your personality in this area by formulating a position and sticking to your opinion in a polite but firm manner. Express the fact that you understand the other person's position but firmly retain your own position without wavering. If people disagree with your position, rather than assume that they disagree with your entire opinion, ask them, instead, what parts of your opinion they don't agree with. If they try to beat you into submission, and you still prefer your own position, just state firmly, "I prefer my position over yours."

The tendency to argue is a personality defect that presents special problems. Many people, by nature, are argumentative. They will argue about anything. If someone says, "Black is black," they will say "You're wrong, black is white and I'll prove it." Arguing is never productive. It simply fuels the fire and tends to polarize people rather than bring them together. If you want to persuade others to your viewpoint, you're better off remaining neutral. If you have developed the arguing habit, and you have a tendency to jump in with both anger and sarcasm, then you will have a real problem in controlling the words that come out of your mouth.

Competitiveness is a personality trait that works for both good and not so good. On one hand competitiveness encourages extra effort. It is the stuff that makes sports great, and competition in business is also great because it gives us better products and lower prices.

On the other hand, competition with your colleagues and personal friends can prove disastrous. It eliminates synergism, under-utilizes skills, and develops uncooperative attitudes. If you find yourself playing the role of a competitor with your associates, then work to eliminate this by competing only with yourself.

The personality problems of people are numerous and complex. I have addressed only a mere fraction of the more common ones. The key to managing your mouth lies in your personality. You can improve your personality by gaining insight into your own quirks and defects and by employing your "growth potential" to overcome them.

## Consider the Source

The role that personality plays in verbal transactions is important. If the speaker is held in high regard, the words mean one thing. If the speaker is held in less than high regard, the words mean something else to the listener. A lot of words are spoken each day. Whether or not the words are heard depends on the source. There is a high correlation between who says the words and how well they are listened to. A person who has earned the respect of others is more likely to be listened to than a person who has not earned respect.

Further, people are more apt to listen to others who they know are successful. This is the basis for testimonial advertisements. Credibility is the key. The line of reasoning is that the successful individual must know something, otherwise he or she wouldn't be a success. Therefore I will listen to what this person has to say and perhaps learn something.

In daily activities, it is often difficult to separate issues from personalities. An issue raised by one person can gain support. The same issue raised by another person can be rejected. Allegiance, friendship, politics, and many other factors influence the sides that people take on issues. The choice is influenced to a great deal by personalities. If you have won the support and respect of your colleagues, then you are much more likely to be listened to when you speak. On the other hand, if you have not won them over, chances are that whenever you say something, your words will fall on deaf ears.

## Controversy

There is a time and a place to be outspoken and thought-provoking. In the corporate world the proper times and places are few and far between. For example, in selling your plans or ideas, about the last thing you would want to do is to create controversy. Controversy, once created, is difficult to diffuse. It usually shoots down plans or ideas before they have a chance to be given a fair hearing or to be properly evaluated. Whether or not the plan or idea has merit no longer matters. What counts is the way the plan or idea impacts on the controversy. Once controversy seeps into any discussion, it usually spells the death knell for the project.

A good management practice is to refrain from introducing new ideas until a preliminary consensus has been gained among the key people who will ultimately decide whether or not to go ahead with the plan or program. If you try to speak out on a particular subject, or introduce a new idea or plan like a bolt from the blue, and you do not have the support elements in place beforehand, you will run the risk of creating controversy.

The way to be successful is to avoid controversy at all costs. Before you propose a new idea, plan, or program, do your homework. Have the facts and documentation at your disposal. Present them one-on-one to the key decision-makers. Get their input. Incorporate it or reject it, but go back to them and explain the reasons for acceptance or rejection. Work things out. When you present your proposal to the group, they will have already bought in and will have an "ownership" position in the program. You present "your" idea with confidence because you know where everyone is coming from, having discussed the whole plan in detail with them. No surprises and no controversy. You win. The payoff is that you get the attention and respect that your work deserves, and you win approval for your idea. If you don't lay the groundwork in advance, you run the risk of creating controversy. Oftentimes the controversy can damage your reputation as well as doom your project. A case in point follows:

\*     \*     \*

During a staff meeting with the top executives of a medium-sized firm, a key manager made a proposal for a new product introduction. He had spent months preparing his facts and figures. He had contacted all the key members of the executive staff except one, the public relations manager. He had purposefully avoided the PR executive as he felt he was totally ineffective, had not really made any contributions to the firm, and was on his way out. At the conclusion of his presentation, the PR executive blurted out, "I don't believe your figures. Are you sure they are correct?"

The manager looked his adversary square in the eye and responded, "If you don't believe my figures, let me see yours and we'll compare them." He had to say it. He could not restrain himself. He knew that the PR executive had no figures. He wanted to take him down a peg. By so doing, he held him up to ridicule in front of the other executives. Even though the other executives realized that the PR executive was an empty suit, they resented the fact that the proposing manager had cut him down in front of all the others.

The manager had shot himself in the foot. The executive group took a different direction. They had been ready to sign off on the project. Now they wanted to debate it. The manager had unwittingly created a forum for controversy.

The controversy had far-flung repercussions. In the case of the manager, his plan was rejected and he damaged his reputation for remaining cool. All his groundwork, although perfectly executed except for the one key figure, the PR executive, was for naught.

The PR executive was fired. The straw that broke the camel's back was that he had blurted out his question without thinking it through. All he accomplished was to make himself look like a fool. He spoke out when he was on shaky ground. He shot from the hip and failed to maintain his professional point of view.

To avoid controversy, you must ensure that you have analyzed, calculated, and studied the issues beforehand so that you are factual and correct. Your effectiveness depends not only on how well you prepare and present your ideas, but how well you can get them implemented. A key to implementing them successfully is to avoid controversy. If you are thoughtful you can envision the sticky points and work to eliminate them.

If you plunk yourself down around the conference table, totally unprepared, and try to wing it based on limited information available at that given moment in the meeting, then you are kidding yourself and you are not a serious player. If you are a serious player, your input will be accepted and will carry weight. If you consistently follow these guidelines, over time your input will be sought and respected. If you are inconsistent, create controversy, shoot from the hip, or present your ideas off the top of your head, you will lose respect. When that happens, your input will not be taken seriously. In the worst case, you will be thought of as an "empty suit."

## Zingers

A personality problem that grows out of aggressiveness and a lack of sensitivity toward others is one that involves a tendency to inflict mental anguish in others. This is accomplished by "zinging" people. Do not zing people. Do not cut them down with one-liners. Before you do, test the situation. Test it by putting yourself in the other person's shoes and asking yourself how you would respond if you were zinged. Would you be happy or would it infuriate you? Would you accept it or would you take issue with it? What would your response be? What would the repercussions be? Would you get hurt by this? How seriously? The problem with zingers is that you have no way of knowing how sensitive others are. A seemingly harmless remark can prove disastrous if the recipient is sensitive. It can backfire on you. Here is a story that illustrates how a simple remark can turn out to be a bad mistake.

One Friday afternoon, in a small company, the sales department was celebrating the achievement of the weekly sales quota. Over the years, whenever a quota was achieved, a bottle or two of champagne was popped and everyone toasted the week's success. Usually employees from other departments popped in and joined in the celebration. The secretary to the VP Sales was a young lady who had recently been hired. She was dedicated to her job and her new boss. Everyone liked her and she had been accepted into the group. She was excited and proud to be part of the celebration.

A manager from another department happened by and joined in the celebration. For want of anything better to say, he singled out the new secretary and blurted out, "Gee, Susie, what are you doing here? Are you old enough to drink?"

Susie went to pieces. Tears welled up in her eyes. She started to cry and left the room. She was overheard to say, "How could he do that to me? He embarrassed me in front of all my friends. I'm old enough to drink. He didn't have to treat me as if I were a child."

The celebration had turned into a disaster. But it didn't end there. The word got back to the president. He called the manager's boss and told him to get his subordinate under control or he was going to fire him. What had started out as a harmless zinger turned out to be a major problem for the offending manager.

## What Goes Around Comes Around

There is absolutely no doubt about it. Information that you initiate and publish will come back and bite you.

Prior to giving out information, consider whether the information will help you to achieve your desired results or will work at cross purposes. Will it help or hinder?

Consider the following. An employee had his wages garnisheed. Each payday, a specified amount of money was deducted from the employee's pay and sent directly to the court. The fact that his wages were garnisheed was confidential. No one knew about it except people in personnel and in the payroll department. The employee was a sales representative. He was hired with the expectation that he would be successful and earn big money. After six months on the job, his performance was dismal and he was not earning any commissions. Of course, the sales manager was concerned. He wondered how long he could keep the rep if he failed to make sales.

Further, the rep's pay was barely enough to keep the individual afloat. During a bull session, a group of managers were discussing sales results, quotas, and how well the sales reps were doing relative to one another. When Jim's name came up, the payroll manager chimed in and said, "Hell, he better start making some sales just so he can cover the deduction that we have to send to the court each week."

When the sales manager heard that, a pained look crossed his face, as if to say, "I didn't know that. What is that all about?" The next time he spoke to the sales rep, he asked him. He shouldn't have, but he did. The sales rep, upon hearing that his boss knew that his wages were being garnisheed, was angry. "That information," he said, "was confidential! It is between me and my creditors. It should not have gotten out. It has nothing to do with my job. I consider this an invasion of privacy."

The employee was right. The payroll department, as represented by the payroll manager, had no business letting that information out. The sales manager did not need to know it. Further, the sales manager did not have to let the sales rep know that he knew it, although that's the way these things work. Once the information is published, you have no way of knowing what will happen. The information that the payroll manager put out came back to bite him. It could have cost the company money and it could have cost the manager his job.

The lesson here is to refrain from making public any

information that does not serve an intended purpose. Further, prior to publishing such information, think it through to the day when it will get back to the person it effects directly, and what that person's reaction will be when he or she hears it.

# Chapter Four

# Special Situations

The flow and control of verbal interaction in special situations such as job interviews or business meetings is vital to your success. Understanding of the process is too important to be left to chance. There are ways to influence and control the outcome, and there are methods and techniques that can increase your awareness and sharpen your skills. The tools necessary for you to be successful are here in this book. All you have to do is understand the concepts, assimilate them, and put them to use.

## Choosing Your Battle Turf

When things don't go your way, it's human nature to get mad. The typical reaction is to do something about it—maybe blow off some steam and get it off your chest. Hold on—don't do it! Restrain yourself. There is a time and a place for everything. The saying "Don't get mad, get even" has a lot going for it. Getting angry and doing what you feel like doing or saying what you feel like saying will not serve your best interests.

A better course of action is to be in control and pick the time and the place to lay your complaint out on the table. Do you sometimes feel it necessary to comment on, challenge, or take issue with everything that comes down the pike? Do you feel compelled to get your two cents in on everything? Don't! Resist the temptation to express yourself on every subject. Learn to say, "So what!" or "What's the big deal?" In other words, bag it. You don't have to get your two cents in on everything. You do not have to let people know what you think on every subject that is brought up. Instead, learn to minimize things, downplay them or dismiss them completely. Here are some rules to go by.

- If it is trivia, treat it as such!
- If it is gossip, dismiss it!
- If it is irrelevant to your situation, ignore it!

Sometimes people feel compelled to respond to stupid remarks or comments just to keep a conversation going. Don't concern yourself with these voids; let someone else grapple with the problem of silence. Avoid the common trap of feeling that the burden is on you to move on. Let someone else bear the burden of continuity. A lot of chatter is better left to die on the vine. Whenever you feel that you are about to be drawn into a meaningless conversation, ask yourself:

- Where is this going?
- Is it worthy of my time?
- Is this a meaningful exchange of information?

A rule of thumb is that if it's small talk to while away the time, it's probably okay. But if someone captures your attention under the pretext that a serious conversation is in order and it turns out otherwise, then tap out and let it die.

## Achilles' Heels

All of us at one time or another have heard horror stories about "slips of the lip"—how good intentions can get fouled up by the unwitting revelation of a vital piece of information at a most unfortunate and inopportune moment. "He let the cat out of the bag" or "she spilled the beans." It's easy to think that a slip of the lip here, a misplaced word there, or a careless remark tossed out won't cause any harm. But you and I know that a remark overheard by the wrong party can get you into deep trouble fast.

Even when you make every effort to control what you say and how you say it, the complex nature of communicating can cause misunderstanding or contradiction or ambiguity. The burden is on you to make sure that the presentation of your message is clearly understood and that the meaning of it is as you intended it to be. The following story illustrates this point.

Jim was asked to provide a courtesy interview for the daughter of a well-known local politician. The president of the firm did not want to hire her. He feared that in the event she failed in the job and was terminated, the politician would have a field day with the company. As a result, he asked Jim to conduct a courtesy interview and get rid of her as tactfully as he could.

It wasn't so easy to get rid of her. The politician had contacted a member of the Board of Directors and convinced him that his daughter should be hired. All the board member had to do was direct the president to do so. The board member called the president and asked him to hire the daughter. The president said he would see what he could do. However, he remained firm in his original position. He did not want her around. He viewed her as a potential problem. She would be a burden when it came to dealing with the many issues that came up within the community, such as environmental control, zoning approvals for plant expansion, traffic flow in and out of the plant, and so on. He told Jim to "interview her and figure out a way to tactfully get rid of her," then added, "I don't want her father's mouth all over me. I don't need it."

Meanwhile the member of the board phoned Jim directly. He directed Jim to make an offer of employment to the daughter and hire her. When Jim relayed that directive to the president, the president became furious. He felt, and rightly so, that the board member had overstepped his bounds and intervened in an operational matter. However, the president was powerless to act. He did not want to incur the wrath of the board member, yet he was more determined than ever to make sure the politician's daughter wasn't hired. His only way out was to have Jim reject her on the pretense that she did not meet the company's needs. The problem lay squarely on the shoulders of Jim. Jim had to get rid of her, and he had to do so in a way that would protect the president and comply with his directive.

Jim did as he was told. He went through the motions. He interviewed the daughter. He rejected her. He told her that he didn't have a suitable position available that she could fit into. Although she was qualified, "her background and experience did not meet the needs of the company." He would, however, "keep her résumé on file," and should something develop, he would establish contact. That, thought Jim, was the end of it. He had done his job and the matter was laid to rest.

About three weeks later, Jim got on the elevator, and the member of the board was standing in the rear. Jim said hello to him. The member returned the courtesy and said hello back. The elevator stopped at the next level and the president got on. Jim and the member each said hello to the president. The president returned the courtesies. As the elevator started to descend, the member of the board said to the president, "Oh, by the way, how is the young lady doing in her new job?" The president turned and replied, "Oh, didn't I tell you, we ended up not hiring her. Jim, here, interviewed her and determined that we didn't have a good match for her. We're waiting for a suitable opening to occur, then we plan to interview her again."

The member responded, "I thought I made myself clear. I asked you to hire her. I don't care if we have a suitable opening or not. Why the hell didn't you do it?"

"I just told you why," the president responded, getting red in the face. "Jim here interviewed her and we didn't have a fit for her."

The member turned to Jim and said, "Jim, you mean to tell me that you couldn't find something for her to do? There must be a dozen jobs that she can fill. Why didn't you hire her? Never mind, don't answer that. I want you to call her up and make her an offer. I don't care what job you give her, just get her on the payroll. Get the picture? Put a copy of the offer letter in my 'in' basket. I'm having lunch with her father and the governor tomorrow, and I want to tell him the good news."

Jim looked at the president. The president gave Jim an icy look. He was miffed. Jim was between a rock and a hard place. He didn't know what to do. In the passion of the moment, he blurted out, "I can't do that! The president doesn't want her around. If something goes wrong with her in the job, her old man's mouth will be all over us."

The president turned red as a beet. The elevator stopped at the first floor and Jim left. Over his shoulder he could see the president and the board member engaged in a heated discussion. Jim had blown it. He didn't sleep that night, and the next day was even worse. He felt that the president had written him off. He was right. Within three weeks, he was history. The politician's daughter was hired. Jim had opened his mouth at the wrong time.

## Bad News Travels Fast

Try getting out news about a key personnel change in your organization. No one pays attention. There are always those that never seem to "get the word." On the other hand, whenever you try to suppress bad news, you find out that the bad news spreads like wildfire.

Why does this happen? The answer is simple. People love to hear about events or happenings that are out of the ordinary. After all, reorganizations, personnel changes, new policies on subjects such as travel and expense reports, are everyday occurrences, but the rumor that the Vice President of Sales has a son at college who was arrested for possession of a controlled substance, aha! That is another matter. That is news! Once put out on the grapevine, it will travel with blinding speed around the circuit.

Bad news travels fast. People want to hear the seamy details, although their reasons may differ. Their motives are unclear. In some cases, they may delight in the fact that it is happening to someone else; in other cases it may make them feel that they have strengthened their position relative to that of the victim and that they have, in a sense, gained the high ground. At least for the moment.

## The Formal Network

In most walks of life there is a formal and an informal network. The *formal network* has been put in place by society to serve a variety of purposes. In business it can be used to communicate information to employees that will make them more effective in their jobs. It can be used for as simple a matter as announcing a promotion or as complex a matter as explaining the position of the company with regard to a major lawsuit or to developing a new product in the marketplace to ward off a threat from the competition.

Whatever use it is put to, the formal network is a managed communications tool. Everything that goes out on it, whether in the community via the mayor's office, in the church from the pulpit, or in the plant or office from management, has been carefully composed, edited, and coordinated to insure that it adheres to policy and expresses the official position of the organization.

Organizations spend millions of dollars to carefully orchestrate their communications programs. From a four-color, slick annual report down to an FYI (For Your Information) memo, you can be assured that every word has been carefully chosen so that there is no room left for misinterpretation. The word that goes out is the exact message that management wants to get out.

I have seen apparently simple and straightforward announcements take as long as ten to twelve weeks to coordinate. Every word was gone over with a fine-tooth comb. In addition, the announcement memos were coordinated with as many as a dozen or so staff people prior to being released. The formal network is alive and well. It is carefully managed and tightly controlled. Whenever you read its bulletins, rest assured that it will transmit exactly what was intended. Very little room will be left open to interpretation by the reader.

# The Informal Network, Alias "The Grapevine"

There is a good reason for calling the informal network a grapevine. A grapevine twists and turns and seems to have no beginning and no end. The information passes from one person to the next, and goes on and on until it spends itself out. It dies only as a result of becoming outdated or irrelevant.

In many ways the *informal network* is more powerful than the formal network. The formal network relies on the written word to ensure that the exact meaning is conveyed. The informal network relies on word of mouth. Word-of-mouth information is subject to wide interpretations and unbridled embellishment as it travels from one person to the next.

The informal network is vastly more effective than the formal network. There are two reasons for this. One reason has already been touched upon—that bad news travels fast, and people are more prone to spread bad news than they are to spread news that deals with routine matters.

The second reason is that people love to talk. We are, by nature, very talkative. Whenever we get the chance, we will strike up a conversation. If there is absolutely nothing new to talk about, then we will talk about the weather. It's a fact, people love to talk, and as a result we yak, chew the fat, and gab about anything under the sun. Because we love to talk, and talking is the natural thing to do, we do not exert much effort over controlling our words. And *that* is the one single factor that causes people to fail. When it comes to the written word, they will edit, erase, change, and draft many copies before they finish their correspondence. When it comes to verbal interaction, they are downright sloppy. Unfortunately, unlike the written word, the spoken words, once said, cannot be erased or called back.

While people usually recognize the importance of what they say, when it can have a negative influence on them, they neglect doing anything about it. Even when they know that what they say is usually what people ultimately judge them by, they pay scant attention to correcting their behavior. Your thinking in this regard must change. It is incumbent upon you to carefully weigh the consequences of your words before you speak them.

## The Job Interview

Can a couple of poorly chosen words spell disaster during a job interview? And how! The landscape of employee recruitment is strewn with the carnage caused by relatively minor mistakes in the use of words. The following story shows how a few misspoken words can turn an otherwise good situation into a disaster:

The president of a large, well-known company was interviewing candidates for a vice president position. The interview was designed to determine whether or not a candidate possessed the necessary background and experience to serve as the focal point for all acquisitions, mergers, and new product development. The requirements were carefully matched against applicants résumés, and only those candidates who possessed the necessary background and experience were invited in for an interview.

After several months of in-depth interviewing, the field had narrowed to two candidates. One candidate was screened out because he balked at the prospect of having to relocate to the East Coast from Chicago. The other candidate was brought in for a final interview with the president. The president wanted to hire the candidate, as he had a number of projects that he wanted to get moving. The offer was contingent on the results of that final interview.

The interview started out on a very positive note. The candidate had met the president's fondest expectations. She had every qualification he could have hoped for, and the interview was in the final stages. The candidate was asked a question dealing with interpersonal skills. She responded by telling the president that her last boss was "an inconsiderate moron who always had to have the last word on every subject," and that he felt that he was always right no matter what the situation.

Well, it wasn't the end of the world, but as far as the president was concerned it gave him a reason to pause and reflect on her character. Why was she spilling out her feelings? Maybe that was the tip of the iceberg. He asked himself, What would she say about me if I did something not to her liking? What other problems will I be buying if I hire her? Her error in judgment proved to be a show stopper. The candidate was screened out and did not get the job.

In retrospect, the CEO could not recall many of the details of the interview. Her background, education, and experience were vague recollections. What did stick in his mind was the fact that the candidate lacked good judgment. She had, in his opinion, committed a cardinal sin. She had dragged dirty laundry out of the closet. Even if her past boss had been as bad as she made him out to be, she should never have criticized him in front of a total stranger, particularly a prospective employer.

The point of this story is that a consistent, almost universally true principle is that the most critical judgments people make about others are based on what has been said. What you say tells the world a story about you. No getting around it, if there is any single clue as to who you really are, that clue lies in your verbal facility. You are what you *say*, and your mouth proves it every day. *You* are the key to your own personality. The plain, old, everyday words that we all take for granted—whether they come out in French, Swahili, or Tonkinese—don't really matter. What does matter is your skill in conveying to your listener the exact meaning of your words and ensuring that no mistakes are made in the process.

Because your words provide clues to your real inner self, they create a mosaic of your personality. They invite critical comparisons, interpretations, and insight by others into the "real" you. As a result, your words shape your image and influence your success. They can make you appear bright, witty, sharp, or eager; they can also make you appear dumb, crude, careless, or unthinking. The words you speak send a message to others that cannot be conveyed in any other way. We've all heard the phrase, "You can dress him up, but you can't take him out." In the real world, it doesn't matter if you look as though you stepped out of *Gentleman's Quarterly* or *Vogue* magazine; simply say a few words that don't click and your image goes down the drain.

## How to Handle a Job Interview Situation

The most critical part of the job-seeking process is the personal interview. When you sit down for that important face-to-face, one-on-one encounter, you are fair game. The interviewer has one objective in mind, and that objective is to find out as much as he or she can about you. The facts are the easiest things to get at. For the most part, your education, experience, salary history, and accomplishments have already been covered on your résumé. A good interviewer won't spend much time belaboring what he or she knows already. Also, chances are your prospective employer had you fill out a job application as well, so the facts relative to your background and experience will have been repeated there. If verification of your education is required, a simple call to the registrar's office with your name and social security number will do the trick. Other facts also can be checked relatively easily.

Instead, the good interviewer will try to get insight into your attitudes, ambition, motivation, intellectual curiosity, and a wide range of personal characteristics that will provide clues to the real you. To get at that information, the interviewer will use a probing strategy that will consist of many different kinds of questions as well as tactics that will get you to open up and reveal your true inner self. The way that you respond to the questions, what you say and how you say it, will often spell the difference between getting the job or getting a "thanks but no thanks" write-off letter.

Okay, finally, after sending out dozens of copies of your résumé and responding to numerous ads, you are invited in for a job interview. Unless you are a professional job hunter, you will find yourself at the mercy of one or more professionals. The first professional you are likely to encounter is the personnel employment specialist. He or she was hired specifically to recruit people. Chances are this person has attended several interviewing seminars and may have screened hundreds of candidates. How are you going to get through the maze? The interviewer will use many skills, tactics, and techniques with you. Let's see how many of them you are familiar with. Answer "yes" or "no" and score one point for each "yes" answer.

1. I am familiar with the technique the interviewer will use to establish rapport.

2. I can differentiate between an open-ended question and a direct question.

3. I have a good idea of the probing strategy the interviewer will use.

4. I can recognize the point at which the interviewer will start to bear down with tough questions.

5. I understand what the interviewer is trying to do by using silence.

6. I understand the technique of "triangularization," which the interviewer may use to get at critical information.

7. I can recognize the formulation and use of hypothesis testing by the line of questions being asked.

8. I understand the interviewer's use of "reflective" and "interpretive" types of questions.

9. I understand the way that my answers to the questions will be interpreted and what will work in my favor and what may work against me.

10. I know how to answer questions so that my intelligence will shine through.

If you scored less than a perfect score, you may not survive a job interview. If you have been going out on job interviews and have not gotten an offer, your lack of understanding of what takes place in a job interview may have hampered you. The following tips are offered to provide you with some insight into the job interview process.

**1. I am familiar with the technique the interviewer will use to establish rapport.**

A good interviewer will start out by establishing a friendly relationship with you. This is called "establishing rapport." The reason it is done is twofold. First of all, the interviewer wants you to be relaxed so that you are comfortable in the interview. Second, the interviewer wants you to be comfortable and relaxed so that you will open up and reveal the information that he or she is seeking.

A good interviewer will not simply ask, "How are you doing today?" or "What's the weather like outside?" No, he or she will put it on a more personal basis and say something like, "That's a nice tie you're wearing" or "I love the color of your blouse." The use of a more personal approach works better for the interviewer. The candidate feels that he has already made a good first impression and is now willing to tell the interviewer everything he wishes to know. That is one way that interviewers will attempt to establish rapport. Your reaction should be one of acceptance of the compliment with the understanding that you are in the hands of a professional and that you must be extremely careful of revealing information that is better left unsaid.

## 2. I can differentiate between an open-ended question and a direct question.

There are a number of different types of questions that an interviewer may use. However, most interviewers will, for the most part, use two types of key questions. One is direct questions—one that can be answered with a simple "yes" or "no." Direct questions generally do not pose any problems.

The other key question most frequently used in interviews is the open-ended question. Open-ended, or indirect, questions are designed to get you to open up and reveal yourself. The interviewer wants you to elaborate. The more information you volunteer the better, as far as the interviewer is concerned. Beware. A word of caution. Don't rattle on! Provide the interviewer with only as much information as is needed to satisfy the question. Do not risk exposing yourself by revealing any information that may be subject to negative interpretation.

When you are asked an open-ended question, you must carefully think through what you are about to say. Under no circumstances should you blurt out the first thing that comes to your mind. Instead, you should try to make points by numbering them. The way this works is as follows. Say, for example, the interviewer asks you, "How do you feel about working for a large company as opposed to a small company?"

Well, you know that the company you are interviewing for is a large company, so your answer will have to be positive with regard to the size of the company. A good answer would be "I like working for a large company for three reasons. The first reason is that a large company provides opportunity for growth and diverse job assignments. Second, I enjoy the prestige associated with working for a large company, having friends, relatives, and colleagues immediately recognize the name of the firm. And finally, I am especially interested in this company because of its excellent reputation."

But you're not off the hook yet. The interviewer may come back at you and say, "True, this is a big company, but you're interviewing with a subsidiary of a large company, and the subsidiary is more like a small company, and we tend to think of ourselves of being somewhat of a mom-and-pop operation."

Now, it would be impossible for you to shift gears and tell the interviewer that you prefer small companies. So what do you do? You carefully think through your answer and decide that you best course of action would be to stick to your original statement and make it clear to the interviewer that you realize the company is a subsidiary and that you feel that the job opportunity represents the best of both worlds. Your response might be as follows: "Yes, I realize that XYZ company is a small subsidiary of giant XYZ corporation. I feel that the opportunity would provide the best of both worlds—being able to join the team in a small organization while at the same time being able to reap the benefits of being a part of a large and prestigious organization such as XYZ corporation."

### 3. I have a good idea of the probing strategy the interviewer will use.

As soon as you sit down with the interviewer, you will be the target for a whole series of questions. The interviewer will go easy in the beginning in order to build up the trusting relationship that he or she started with a compliment early on. Questions are never asked in a vacuum. There is usually a line of questioning that the interviewer has developed as a guide to how the interview will be conducted. This is referred to as a probing strategy.

The experienced interviewer will ask basic questions early on in the interview. Questions such as "Tell me about the area that you grew up in," "When did you make the decision to attend college?" "How did you arrive at that decision?" As the interviewer gets deeper into the interview, the questions will become more specific to the job for which you are being interviewed. If you are to be successful, you have to be able to anticipate where that line of questioning is going. For example, if the interviewer asks you where you expect to be five years from now, you can rest assured that his next question may be "What are you doing to get there?" followed up by a third question, which may be "What will you do if you don't get there?"

### 4. I can recognize the point at which the interviewer will start to bear down with tough questions.

The transition from the simple questions to the hard questions is easy to recognize. The experienced interviewer knows that you have ready-made, established answers for the easy questions. Questions that deal with your past employment have answers waiting in the wings. Long ago you developed an explanation for the gap in your employment. The reasons for leaving jobs are down pat. Your slow salary growth and any other problem areas in your track record have been carefully thought through and you are prepared with the proper answer. Right? The transition to the tough questions begins when the interviewer starts to ask about how you will apply your background and experience to the position for which you are being interviewed.

To answer those questions effectively, you will have to do your homework. You must know such things as the line of business that your prospective employer is engaged in; the competition in the industry; the specific skills, experience, and knowledge that the job will require; where the job fits into the organization; and a wide range of other very specific facts pertinent to the job. When that line of questioning starts, you must be prepared to answer the questions in terms that will indicate to the employer that you have the knowledge and confidence to do the job.

The only way that you can make that happen is to do your homework up front. Find out as much as you can about the company and the job so that you can answer the tough questions intelligently. Do not try to wing it. You will be doomed from the start. Don't ask any questions that will betray your lack of knowledge about the position. And don't make any remarks that are not grounded in factual information. Your answers will have to convince the employer that your experience is exactly the kind of experience that is necessary in order to succeed in the position, and that you are a "good fit" for the opening. Anything short of that and you're out!

### 5. I understand what the interviewer is trying to do by using silence.

At various times during the interview, the interviewer may deliberately remain silent. Rather than ask you a question to get the interview going again, there will be a pregnant pause. This is known as using the technique of silence, and it is designed to get you to take the lead in the interview. Do not take the lead by volunteering more information. Rather, use the pause as an opportunity to ask the interviewer good questions. The questions should be relevant to the company and the position. Questions dealing with personal considerations, such as working conditions or benefits, are taboo and under no circumstances should they be broached during the preliminary hiring interviews. If the company is interested in you, all of that information will be provided to you in the form of brochures and so on.

### 6. I understand the technique of "triangularization," which the interviewer may use to get at critical information.

As you go through the interview, the interviewer may sense that you are holding back vital information. The more you are questioned in a particular area, the more evasive you become. The sharp interviewer, realizing that he or she is getting less and less information and that you are becoming more and more uneasy, will drop the line of questioning for the time being. However, be assured that the interviewer will revert to the same line of questioning using different words and a different approach. This is known as triangularization.

For example, let's assume that you left your last job because your performance was not what it should have been. You told the interviewer that you left your position due to a cutback. As the interviewer questions you about the size of the cutback, you are evasive about the number of people involved. You would like him to believe that it was a large cutback and that you were one of many people let go at the same time. The truth of the matter is that only a handful of people were let go and most of them because of performance. The company had "cleaned house" under the guise of a reduction in force in order to get rid of some dead wood, and you were included in that pile. Through the process of triangularization, the interviewer will come at you from a different direction in order to get at the true situation. The best defense against this line of questioning is to say as few words as possible, and stick by your original story. That is, you were let go as a result of a reduction in force. As far as the numbers go, you are not sure, as you did not know the overall company program.

## 7. I can recognize the formulation and use of hypothesis testing by the line of questions being asked.

As the interviewer starts to bear down on you, the questions will get tougher and more penetrating. The interviewer knows that most applicants are like the tip of an iceberg. They will reveal only a small portion of themselves. The interviewer understands that and will work on getting you to open up by continually making and testing assumptions about you. The interviewer forms a hypothesis based on something in your résumé or in your application. Here is the way that works.

Let's assume that you are applying for a position as a sales representative. The sales representative position requires a great deal of initiative. The interviewer formulates a hypothesis like this: This candidate is not a self-starter but rather needs to be closely supervised in order to produce. Using that hypothesis, the interviewer will construct a series of questions. The answers to those questions will either support or reject the hypothesis.

Hypothesis testing forms the basis for most of the questioning that goes on in a job interview. The way that you respond to the questions that are being thrown at you will work either for you or against you. In order to make sure that you understand this concept so that you will be able to recognize what is behind the interviewer's questions, let me give you another example.

A candidate is seeking a position as a marketing manager. She has a bachelor's degree in marketing and is working toward her MBA. She soon finds out that there is a "catch-22" involved in her career. She can't get a job as a marketing manager because she doesn't have any experience, and she can't get the experience because she doesn't have a marketing job. So what does she do? How can she get her foot in the door? She applies for a job as a secretary. She knows that once she gets the job as a secretary, within a year or two she should be able to transfer into a professional position through the company's internal promotion program.

During the course of the interview for the secretarial position, the interviewer formulates the hypothesis that this candidate, with her bachelor's degree in marketing, is not really looking for a career as a secretary but rather is using the secretarial position as a stepping stone. Even though that kind of career strategy may be commendable, the personnel manager doing the hiring wants to cut down on secretarial turnover and truly wants secretarial candidates that will remain secretaries for a reasonable period of time. Armed with that hypothesis, the interviewer formulates a whole series of questions and bombards the applicant from every direction.

If the applicant knows what tactic is being employed, then she can withstand the bombardment and get the job. Here is where being able to manage your mouth pays off, and here is what you do in this situation. You formulate your own strategy. Your strategy is, in effect, as follows: Regardless of how many times the interviewer tries to find out what my career intentions are, I will tell him or her that I desire to be a secretary. If the interviewer asks me how long I want to be a secretary, I will respond, "Indefinitely." If he or she asks me why I want to be a secretary, I will respond, "I like the work, the challenge, and the hours." Regardless of what kinds of questions I am asked, I will stick to my story and convince the interviewer that I truly want the secretarial job for which I am applying and have no underlying motives. As tempted as I may be to open my mouth and tell the interviewer how much I would like to use my marketing degree, I will bite my tongue and stick to my story. I will swallow my pride and get into the company the best way, and perhaps the only way, that I know how.

## 8. I understand the interviewer's use of "reflective" and "interpretive" types of questions.

Reflective questions are used to get you to open up. They can be very effective, so be alert to their use. A reflective question consists of repeating or rephrasing a portion of what you say. For example, suppose you say, "And then things sort of fell apart at my last job. My boss and I were constantly having a tug of war."

The interviewer will definitely want to know more about your so-called tug-of-war, so he or she will reflect the question by saying, "You had disagreements with your boss?" If you're not careful, you will be sucked in and will provide more detail about your disagreements. Needless to say, you will be shooting yourself in the foot. The way to avoid this trap is to refrain from giving out any negative information. Once you give the interviewer the slightest opening, you can rest assured that he or she will charge in with both guns blazing.

Interpretive types of questions are somewhat trickier. The interviewer will go beyond what you have said and interpret your response. He or she will piece together what you have said and add something to it. In that fashion, the interviewer hopes to move deeper into the subject. For example, the interviewer might say, "Could it be that you and your supervisor were having tugs-of-war because he was promoted over you?" Obviously, to make such an interpretation the interviewer had to piece together many fragments of the interview. If, however, his interpretation is correct, then you are going to have a tough time getting around that question. The way to deal with this situation is to remain calm. Do not tense up or get defensive. If the interpretation is correct, you can minimize its impact by saying something like, "Yes, he was promoted over me. He is a good supervisor, however, and I have learned a great deal from him. Our occasional tugs-of-war were just the ordinary give-and-take involved in getting our mission accomplished. Basically, we get along great and we have a great deal of respect for one another." The next time around, don't leave any room for interpretation or you may find yourself with a noose around your neck.

9. **I understand the way that my answers to the questions will be interpreted and what will work in my favor and what may work against me.**

Every time the interviewer asks a question, he or she will be listening intently for your response. The interviewer will also be looking for the nuances or gestures that can alter or shade the meaning of the spoken words. Your inflection, tone of voice, body language, facial expression, and choice of words will either add to or subtract from the credibility of your responses.

The job of the interviewer is to evaluate the data that is

collected on you during the course of the interview. A major source of error that the evaluator is exposed to is his or her personal biases. It is human nature to make judgments about people even though the exposure to them has been for only a short period of time.

General impressions and subjective judgments may play a minor part in the overall evaluation, but they do play a part. Therefore you must make every effort to ensure that you score high in those departments as well as in the factual data department. Your first impression is important, and even though it is not related to the job requirements, it behooves you to make a good one. However, as was pointed out earlier, the first impression, though hard to overcome, won't last long, and what comes out of your mouth will form the basis for the judgment passed on you.

Interviewers tend to focus more on the negatives than on the positives. One negative can offset ten positives. You must eliminate the negatives or at least keep them to an absolute minimum. Try to win over the interviewer. The best way to do this is to articulate well, maintain your poise, and state your answers clearly and concisely.

**10. I know how to answer questions so that my intelligence will shine through.**

Make sure that your responses meet the following criteria: One, they are grammatically correct. Two, they specifically address and respond to the question that was asked. Three, they are devoid of slang, trite expressions, colloquial words or phrases, or curse words, which may detract from your professionalism. Four, they come across as sincere. Five, they display your intelligence. This can best be accomplished by answering questions in a one, two, three format. For example, in the first place, in the second place, and finally, in the third place, and so on.

In summary, if you are to be successful in a job interview, then you must use your interpersonal skills to the best advantage. As the interviewer gathers data on you, he or she will be continually making judgments. Every word that comes out of your mouth is critical to your success. You can be successful if you use the right words and make sure that your diction, timing, and delivery enhance them. Your object is to create a positive impression that depicts you as possessing the values, personality, traits, and characteristics that add up to success.

## What! Another Meeting?

Meetings, by definition, involve people. In most companies meetings are a way of life. There are the Monday morning staff meetings, lunch meetings, weekly review meetings, operating review meetings, budget meetings, sales meetings, meetings to schedule meetings. On and on they go, one meeting after another. Some meetings are short and some are long. Some are important and others are a waste of time.

From an individual's career development standpoint,

some good can be derived from every meeting that is attended. You can enhance your position in the organization by managing what you say and how you say it. The subject matter of the meeting will no doubt be soon forgotten, but the way you conducted yourself will leave an indelible imprint on the other attendees.

## Meeting Behavior

Let's take a closer look at meeting behavior and how you can profit by it. But first let's take an inventory of our meeting skills. Please identify the following statements as "true" or "false" as they apply to *you*.

1. I speak at meetings only when I am called to speak.

2. I rarely put any ideas on the table.

3. I try to answer completely and honestly all questions that are put to me.

4. I rarely ask any questions of others at meetings.

5. I rarely support any ideas unless they come from the boss.

6. I rarely if ever pick up on others' ideas and lend support.

7. I do not feel that I contribute much at meetings.

8. I prefer to let others do the talking.

9. I feel that I am missing a great deal at meetings,

whereas others seem to know what's going on at all times.

10. I do not feel that meetings should be used for problem solving, as the problems generally are too complex for easy answers.

11. I never disagree with anything that is said at a meeting, even when I know it is wrong.

12. When confronted in a meeting, I will back down rather than stand my ground.

13. I would never call anyone's bluff in a meeting, even when I know someone's ideas are half-baked.

14. I would never try to railroad another's idea in front of others.

15. I prefer to deal with nasty situations in a one-on-one encounter.

16. When I don't understand something, I let it slip by rather than ask for clarification and appear stupid.

Do people behave the same way in meetings that they do in a one-on-one situation? No! They do not. As you can probably see from the above self-test, you have a great many more inhibitions in a meeting than you would have in a one-on-one situation. Two individuals speaking to just each other usually conduct themselves in a calm, cordial, friendly, and understanding manner. If you inject a third party into the meeting, invariably the third person will side with one or the other of the original participants, and the whole tenor of the meeting will change. Now that the odds are 2–1, the lone participant will become more defensive and the other two will start to exhibit more aggressive behavior. Add a fourth person to the group, and totally different behavior will ensue.

The size of the group will start to inhibit everyone, and words that would have flowed easily will now become harder to get out as the inhibitions set in. Add a few more people to the group and the dynamics will change again. Mix the group up and inject the presence of the boss, and a totally different meeting will ensue.

With the boss now present, the participants will say quite different things than they would if their boss was not there. The group behavior will suddenly become more predictable as everyone starts to toe the line and defer to the boss for leadership. Rest assured, no one will speak his or her mind. The freewheeling conversation that was occurring in the one-on-one meeting has now given way to a highly ordered group meeting wherein the organization's power structure dictates the mood and the future course of the meeting. No doubt you have heard the expression "Hold off until you have the proper forum." The proper forum is dependent on the size and makeup of the group. Size and makeup determine the politics—who will be on what side, how the players will line up with one part of the group or the other.

Groups are used for many vital functions. During a group meeting you can build consensus, reach an agreement, sell an idea, make a decision, coordinate activities, and team build. Unfortunately, very little time is spent on work activity. In many cases a lot of time is spent on fighting, bitching, brown nosing, maneuvering, manipulating, apple polishing, and politicking. Many times the issues on the table get buried, achieving the group objectives gets lost in the shuffle, and the participants leave the meeting scratching their heads. "What was that all about?" they ponder.

In situations like that, it behooves you to know how to survive and thrive on that kind of meeting. After all, very little if anything will actually get done, but you can reap some return from the meeting by handling yourself well. Let's take a closer look at the dynamics of a group meeting.

Your effectiveness in a group situation depends upon your exhibiting the proper behavior. To be at your best in a group meeting you have to understand the dynamics of the meeting and what role people are playing. The breakdown of the various behavior outlined earlier will assist you in that regard. If you understand where people are coming from and where they are going, you will be better equipped to manage your own behavior during the course of the meeting. Try answering the following questions:

1. From your own experience, do you feel that people fall into distinct categories?

2. Are there low contributors and high contributors?

3. Are there a few information givers and many information seekers?

4. Does one person always seem to be blocking or disagreeing?

5. What about you? Are you a contributor? To what degree?

Did you ever test understanding during a meeting? Not too many people do; they just assume everyone is listening and understanding. At the next meeting you attend, observe what is going on. Analyze who is attacking, who is defending, who is proposing, and who is testing understanding by asking for clarification, amplification or examples. Check your own behavior and ask yourself if you can improve on it.

Good meeting skills, in my experience, are those that seek information, build, support, test understanding, and summarize. The controversial behavior includes disagreeing, defending, and blocking.

Many different kinds of behavior have their place in meetings. The critical point that you must bear in mind involves separating the short-term problems that come up in the meeting from the longer-range goals that you aspire to.

The stakes that are being played for in a group meeting are on two levels. Some of the players are actually trying to problem solve. Other, more astute players are developing their posture in the organization. These motives help explain the behavior that will be exhibited by the players. Your main concern should be directed toward developing your posture. The issues will be resolved outside the meeting, most likely in a one-on-one meeting between the people that are directly impacted by the issue.

As far as you are concerned, the real stake in the meeting is how you will be perceived as a result of how you handle yourself. I said it before and I will say it again. Long after the issues are forgotten, the behavior that was exhibited will remain in everyone's mind. Indelibly!

## Meeting Skills

To begin with, all professionals need meeting skills. Research indicates that as you progress up the ladder of success, you will be attending meetings on a regular basis. The skills needed for success in meetings are an extension of one-on-one interpersonal skills. In a meeting they become even more critical. The one meeting skill that stands out is the one that requires you to retain control over your thought processes so that you don't run the risk of laying your thoughts out on the table for everyone to see. You must control your words during meetings, and the words you do use must work for you in your best interest.

Meeting effectiveness depends on not only what you say and how you say it, but also how the others interpret it. It is true that oftentimes the things you say are more important than the things you do. Your credibility depends on your mouth. When you say something, is it true? Is it the "truth, the whole truth, and nothing but the truth"? Or is it half-true, partially true, or only a teensy bit true? Do you have credibility with your colleagues? Credibility is hard to come by nowadays. It is very elusive.

People say what others expect to hear. They say self-serving things and grind their own axes. Few people speak their minds in meetings. Why? Most likely because it is usually risky to do so and can be costly in terms of your standing in the group.

In the course of a meeting, some people will overstate their cases and others are masters of the understatement. It doesn't take long to find out whom to believe and whom not to. If you say something once and it turns out not to be true, then you are usually given the benefit of the doubt. If you say something on another occasion, and that, too, turns out to be untrue, then you have two strikes against you. At that point, anything further that you say will be questionable. What is at stake is your credibility. If people are to believe you, then you must carefully analyze what you are about to say to ensure that it is as accurate as it can be. This means that you cannot cut corners or fill in the gaps with conjecture or take other shortcuts. You can't fabricate things and pass them off as facts. You must speak the truth. If you cannot speak the truth, then you must use other tactics such as skirting the issue or employing one or more of the techniques that we will cover in a later chapter.

Conducting yourself well in a meeting depends on your verbal skills. Do you say the right thing at the right time? Do the things you say adhere to the philosophies of your coworkers? Do you recognize who your friends are during a business meeting and who your adversaries are? Does your tone, inflection, and choice of words stay within the realm of the situation? If not, you've got a lot of work ahead of you to improve your meeting skills. The following is a case in point.

During the course of a management meeting, the discussion became very heated. There were three or four issues at stake and the management team had broken up into factions. Positions had polarized and the discussion became heated. Arguments broke out. Several managers lost their tempers. They flared up. Expletives were shouted. One manager threatened to inflict bodily harm on another.

Several months after that meeting, many of the participants could not remember what the issues were that everyone got upset over. Every person, however, remembered the excessive behavior of the participants. During that meeting, the images of several managers were damaged. One manager's image sunk to a new low, and as long as he stayed with the company, he never recovered fully from that incident.

After the meeting, the grapevine took over and the word went out.

"So-and-so is a low-life roughneck."

"I will never believe another word that he says."

"Did you hear the things he said about Ralph? I wouldn't treat a dog like that."

"That guy is bad news. I will never again deal with him on the same basis as I would prior to that meeting. How anyone could sink that low is beyond me."

The meeting was a disaster for that manager. Did anyone remember the issues? Probably one or two, but the behavior overshadowed everything else. And no doubt, a year from the meeting no one would remember the issues but practically everyone would remember the behavior. What really matters is that you be on guard to insure that at least three things happen when you find yourself in a tough spot. First of all, you must realize that your behavior will be remembered by everyone. You want that memory to be positive and complimentary to your image. Second, know that your effectiveness as a manager is at stake and that your behavior plays a major part in gaining the respect of your colleagues so that you can assume a leadership role in the organization. Finally, realize that the achievement of your own objectives and the successful implementation of your plans and ideas are the sum of the first two factors. Your success or failure in achieving your objectives depends on your behavior, which in turn influences your co-workers to perceive you as a professional.

# Chapter Five
# How to Deal with Gossip

When it comes to gossip, just about every human being is guilty of having participated in it at one time or another. Although women have generally taken the rap as the prime offenders, men are just as guilty. Gossipy people are found everywhere, in all walks of life, all ages, throughout the world. Nothing is sacred anymore. Everything and everyone is fair game. Politicians, the clergy, heads of state, the rich and famous, you name them, they are all targets. The media sniffs them out and nails them on the six o'clock news. From then on . . . wham! Instant notoriety! So, you may ask, how do I deal with it? The answer to that question is twofold. First, you need to ground yourself in a solid understanding of what gossip is and the many faces that it has. Second, you need to know how to deal with it in its many forms so that you won't fall victim to it, either as the target or as a participant.

## Gossip

Human nature, being what it is, loves gossip. A lot of gossip. A lot of scandal. We have a high need to dish the dirt, and we have a great preoccupation with who is in love with whom, who is sleeping with whom, who is straight, who is gay, who is getting divorced, who has contracted AIDS, who uses dope, and all the rest. Old and young alike delight in telling and hearing the stories that make the rounds in their circle of friends.

True, society dictates that you maintain a certain level of respectability. Everyone knows what people are supposed to do, and what they are not supposed to do. Gossip affirms the mores of the community and reassures the inhabitants that any transgressions against those mores will be countered by the force of gossip. Advocates of gossip as a force for controlling human behavior put forth the argument that if you do something wrong, then you should be exposed and everyone should know about it. In that way, you will keep yourself in control. Do something wrong, the word goes out and everyone learns of your transgression. The fear of other people finding out about our misbehavior inhibits us and keeps us in check. But gossip does a lot more damage than good. It is definitely a force for evil. Let's see why.

## Ha Ha ! That's a Riot!

The American public relishes the jokes that go around in the wake of someone's personal disaster. Many of the jokes grow out of malicious gossip, rumors or hearsay. And the more the accused tries to defend his or her position, the worse it gets. No matter what the subject is, no matter what is held up in the courts, if it gets to that, no matter whether the rumors are founded or unfounded, the subject quickly becomes the butt of the jokes.

Jokes are often dirtier or more vicious than the actual rumors, and usually more devastating. The joke serves as a vehicle for spreading the rumor. The rumor spreads with a speed that is astonishing. A joke that starts in New York can travel around the world in minutes, in about the same amount of time it takes Joe Smith to tell his business associate in Hong Kong. An executive in the shipping industry, in describing the gossip situation in her industry, likened it to a "bunch of cackling old women." The nature of the industry is such that all transactions require global communications in order to track the whereabouts of ships at all times throughout the far corners of the world. The people that operate the communications systems have over the years developed close bonds of friendship, even though they have never met face-to-face.

Over the years they have gained each other's confidence and trust to the point where the network has become a modern-day version of the old rural party-line telephone system. The participants trade gossip on a daily basis. Instead of the usual one-on-one conversation, they utilize global wire services and long-distance telephone calls. Gossip in the shipping industry gets out within the hour, to the entire world.

## Idle Talk

"Idle talk" connotes a nice, chatty kind of dialogue. Two people get together and swap tales. They bandy the information around and talk about trivial or relatively unimportant matters. Who's been shining up to the boss, or who is in the office clique and who is out. Sounds innocent enough. What harm can come out of that? Whatever form gossip takes in its early stages, it is sure to escalate rapidly as the bond between the practitioners strengthens. From an initial exchange of innocent or neutral information, the process tends to feed on itself, and soon the two move from the idle talk stage to serious gossip. The insidious nature of gossip does not allow its practitioners to fully understand its destructive nature. The participants view it as play with an element of mischief. The history of mankind, however, has a different viewpoint. From the earliest days of recorded history up to the present, gossip has been with us. Let's take a look at what the scriptures have to say about it.

## The Bible Tells Us So

In the New Testament, we find a reference that tells us that one of mankind's shortcomings falls under the heading of "abuses of the tongue."

The Bible tells us:

> If anyone is never at fault in what he says, he
> is a perfect man, able to keep this whole body in
> check.

> When we put bits into the mouths of horses to
> make them obey us, we can turn the whole an-
> imal. Or take ships as an example. Although
> they are so large and are driven by strong winds,
> they are steered by a very small rudder wherever
> the pilot wants to go. Likewise the tongue is a
> small part of the body, but it makes great boasts.
> Consider what a great forest is set on fire by a
> small spark. The tongue also is a fire, a world of
> evil among the parts of the body. It corrupts the
> whole person, sets the whole course of his life
> on fire, and is itself set on fire by hell.

> All kinds of animals, birds, reptiles and crea-
> tures of the sea are being tamed and have been
> tamed by man, but no man can tame the tongue.
> It is a restless evil, full of deadly poison.

> With the tongue we praise our Lord and Fa-
> ther, and with it we curse men, who have been
> made in God's likeness. Out of the same mouth
> come praise and cursing. My brothers, this
> should not be. Can both fresh water and salt
> water flow from the same spring? My brothers,

can a fig tree bear olives, or a grapevine bear figs? Neither can a salt spring produce fresh water.

## Bad News

Gossip is not a respectable pastime. Carried out under an umbrella of secrecy between two close friends at the outset, it snowballs and in the end causes everyone a great deal of harm. From an intimate conversation between two close friends, the information travels the same way any social disease does, from one lover or friend to another lover or friend.

Originally the word "gossip" meant a godparent, a companion or a crony. Over the years the definition of the word has changed, and it has now come to mean a person who habitually reveals personal or sensational facts of an intimate nature.

So why do people gossip? If it's bad, why do they do it? Most of us know from experience that it is bad. It is the source of much discontent in human relations. It goes against our value system, and our values are deeply held. They constitute the backbone of our beliefs. However, we tend to put them aside when it comes to gossip, and we persist in participating in it. Why is this so? What is wrong with our value system when it comes to gossip? Why does it break down? What is the cause of this inconsistency? Let's take a closer look at it.

Our values evolve from our experience. They influence everything we do. They are often culturally based, broadly held, and very slow to change. Our values influence what we strive for, how we act, and how we establish our goals in life. They determine what we set out to do and what we decide not to do. Yet, when it comes to gossip, we have a tendency to put our values aside and indulge in it. Again, why do we do this? What is there about gossip that is so alluring that we get seduced into participating in it?

For one thing, most normal human beings value the same things. We derive self-esteem from being in control of our actions. We pride ourselves on being able to control our outward appearance. We know how to react to the daily highs and lows of living. Our behavior is generally uniform and predictable. We want to be perceived as steady, solid citizens in control of our emotions. We dread overreacting to any given situation, and we strive to remain calm and cool under fire or in the face of adversity. To do all these things, we rely on self-discipline to pull us through.

Deep down inside, however, we have a tendency to unconsciously pick and choose when and where we will apply our values. We react to those around us and keep our options open. We readily shift our values to accommodate the situation. Especially so when the fear of alienating others is present. This flexible value system is intentional. It results from thinking and acting in a basically simple manner, that of going with the flow.

In one-on-one chats with close friends, the situation does not require any defense mechanisms to be in place. The pair trust each other totally. They are bonded together. More important, they can compromise their value systems and get away with it. There is a little bit of larceny in everyone, and if one feels that he or she can get away with something, usually he or she will try to.

So, in that kind of a situation, where one friend most certainly will not chastise another friend, what they say to each other is kept between the two of them. When they spread the story, and they will, it will, of course, be handled the same way between the next pair of friends or confidants. The participants will be open and honest with one another. All others are fair game. They are not on the same terms with the two sharing information. They are outsiders. The two friends will shed their layers of objectivity, professionalism, coolheadedness, and rock-solid values and indulge one another by revealing their innermost thoughts and secrets as they revel in childlike mischief.

Oddly enough, as they reveal their mischievous substructure, they take pleasure in it, despite the cost to others. It's cruel, but they enjoy it. They know that the mischief they create and revel in will not come back to haunt them. So they are relatively immune from any repercussions. As a result, when it comes to gossip, it is very difficult to put an end to it. People are all too willing to short-circuit their value system and indulge in it. Knowing that they will not suffer any repercussions, they have nothing to lose. Until, of course, they fall victim to the process.

## Incubation

As we have established, in order for gossip to take place, there must exist a warm friendship between two people.

Usually the friendship has developed over a long period of time, so it is solid. That long-term association sets the stage for the warmth and privacy that is needed in order to share information of a personal nature. The kinship that develops from the association allows for that to take place. The conversations are underscored by trust, friendship, and confidence in one another, and a mutual understanding is resident in both parties that they are the only two who will ever share the same information.

In the event that one passes it on to another, the source of the information will forever remain obscure. That special relationship, with its built-in ground rules, sets the stage for intimate conversation. It is the incubator without which gossip could not thrive, much less exist.

## The Many Faces of Gossip

Gossiping is unbelievably simple and, at the same time, overwhelmingly complex! As we have said, in its simplest form, it involves two people talking about a third person. The two people share a close bond. They exchange intimate knowledge about the third person. They can speak freely and openly because they trust one another not to reveal the content of their conversation or the source of their information to anyone else. If any outside interference is encountered, the gossip ceases. Gossip, in order to be gossip, mandates that the sanctity of the conversation remain intact. If, for example, a third person happened by and joined in the conversation, the conversation would change. The subject would abruptly shift to a different topic, and the third person would not have the foggiest idea what the other two had been talking about when he or she approached them.

When the third party departs, the gossip may pick up where it left off. That's the way it is! And from a simple one-on-one intimate conversation on a relatively obscure subject to a full-blown, worldwide scandal, the elements of gossip are the same. Only the magnitude varies. Let's take a look at the kinds of gossip that are routinely present in our everyday encounters.

## Garden-Variety Gossip

In everyday, garden-variety gossip, old and young delight in telling about all the little incidents that go on in town. This goes on over the backyard fence, during bridge club, or during little chitchats at each other's homes. No story is ever too trivial to stir up an active response from the participants. As harmless as this seems, it sets in motion an exaggeration of the details of the situation and an embellishment of those details by active imaginations. In general, garden-variety gossip tends to deal with nonthreatening subjects. Given the chance, however, it can soon develop into malicious gossip, bent on the destruction of other human beings.

## Malicious Gossip

In its worst form, the information contained in gossip can be malicious. It reeks of half-truths and lies and casts an unfavorable light on reputations. People relish hearing about others' misfortunes or escapades. Anything that happens to a person or is found out about a person that is outside the realm of normal behavior or the mores of society is ripe for becoming the subject of malicious gossip. Unfortunately, many of us have been on the receiving end. And we know all too well how painful that can be. Many a life has been ruined or destroyed by malicious gossip, and irreparable harm has been wreaked on humanity.

If you are to be successful in managing your mouth, an important element in that process is to first understand what gossip is and then understand why people engage in it. If these two elements are understood, then your heightened awareness will stand you in good stead when you are confronted with a situation that has the earmarks of a gossip session. Hopefully you will back away from it and by so doing nip it in the bud.

But beware, gossip has an aura of temptation surrounding it. It is like a big, fat piece of chocolate cake that is placed in front of you when you are on a diet. You know you shouldn't eat it, but what the heck, why not, it tastes so good. Gossip is like that piece of cake. If you are to be successful you will have to exercise self-control. It is every bit as tempting to indulge in as it is to wolf down the cake. With gossip, however, you don't have to worry about calories (only your reputation).

## Office Gossip

A Stamford, Connecticut, firm had a new Vice President of Sales. His name was Judd. He had been on the job for eight months. He was hired through an executive search firm. In his former position, he was a VP of Sales for a Chicago-based firm. As part of his compensation package, he was offered real estate relocation assistance.

One day, two of the VP's direct reports were talking to each other. One was a sales manager and the other was Manager, Advertising and Sales Promotion. The sales manager had a worried look on his face. When asked by the Manager, Advertising and Sales Promotion why he looked so worried, he responded, "I was just chatting with Judd, and for some reason I get the feeling that all is not well with him. So much so in fact that I will bet you a dollar to a doughnut that he doesn't move his family from Chicago to Connecticut." "Why do you think that?" the ad manager asked. "I don't know, I just have a gut feeling." "If that's all you have to go on, I will take you up on the bet."

Later that week, the VP Sales approached the human resources manager and asked, "What's going on? Everyone that I speak to asks me how I'm doing. I feel that I have a terminal disease. I get the feeling that they know something that I don't." "It's the rumors," the human resources manager replied. "The grapevine has it that you are not committed to the job and that you have no intention of moving your family and making a go of it." "A go of it! You make it sound as if I am failing. Am I?"

The human resources manager responded, "I'll level with you. No, you're not failing, but it appears that you're dragging your feet in finding a house and moving your family. That tells the world that you are not serious about sticking with us. Otherwise you would have bought something and settled in by now." "That's utterly ridiculous, I am closing on a house in two weeks and my family has already moved out of the house in Chicago, and they are staying with her mother until the new house is ready. God, how do these rumors get started?"

The ad manager lost a doughnut. Unfortunately the company lost a lot more. The loss on the part of the company was in valuable work time, concentration on the mission, dissension, and a sapping of productivity and morale. Gossip in the work place has a strong effect on how well and how much people produce. Productivity suffers because gossip eats up work time and damages the welfare and morale of the employees. Office gossip can be kept to a minimum if you approach it from the standpoint that it is a management problem and as such should be treated the same as any other problem. Several problem-solving steps can be taken to get it under control. Find out what people are talking about. Observe what is going on in the work place. Who talks to whom. Are there certain groups of people that always seem to be in a huddle? Do they congregate in any one spot? Someone's office or in the lunchroom at the same table? Make it your business to stop, look, and listen to find out who the main players are in the office grapevine. Ask questions about gossip. Let people know that you are interested in hearing about how much time is being lost by passing stories around. You may be surprised at the answers you get. Develop an awareness in your employees as to the inherent bad that can come from office gossip.

This can be done in training sessions, as part of staff meetings, or by posters on the bulletin boards. The more that people know and understand the dangers, lost productivity, and effect on morale that result from gossip, the more likely they are to avoid it.

Have your managers set the example. The old saying, that a fish stinks from the head down, is an appropriate one. If the top people in the company can't refrain from gossiping, how do they expect their subordinates to do so?

## Avoiding Temptation

To provide some guidance in helping to control our tendency to indulge in gossip, let us set the stage with a short scenario.

Mary and Bill work for a medium-sized company. Mary is young, attractive, and single. She is the executive secretary to the president. Bill is around forty, married, with three children. In the past week both Mary and Bill have been the subjects of gossip. The stories circulating about them were unrelated. They involved two separate and distinct situations. With regard to Bill, the story was that he had a drinking problem, which in turn caused him to have marital troubles. This, in turn, was affecting his performance on the job. Mary was perceived as spending far too much time behind closed doors in the president's office. Further, last week she and the president went on a business trip together. It was a three-day trip to a trade show convention in Las Vegas. It was highly unusual for the president to take a secretary along. He had never done anything like that in the past. He had been president for ten years and he was held in high regard by all the employees as a pillar in the community. The stories making the rounds went like this:

"Hey, Charley, don't tell anyone I told you, but Bill is in real trouble. Yeah, take it from me. He is in real trouble. Not only has he been boozing it up, but now even his old lady is fed up with him. I also heard he's not doing too well on the job."

"Well, Ed, let me tell you one. Notice anything funny about Mary lately? She looks like the cat that swallowed the canary. I think the boss is boffing her. Did you know that she went to Vegas with him for the convention? Three days in the fun and sun. Trade shows are bad enough with all the loose action around, but imagine taking your secretary along. Especially a knockout like Mary. Something must be going on. Every time I pass the boss's office, Mary's not at her desk and the boss's door is closed. Is she in there with the boss? What are they doing? Don't they know that employees aren't stupid and that they can put two and two together? And what if this gets upstairs to top management? They will come down hard on them. And what if this gets back to the boss's wife. This could be the start of a major catastrophe for this business. Things are getting out of hand around here. What are we supposed to do?"

In this situation, the gossip chain has begun. Soon it will be all over the company and the community. The gossip consists of information that may be real, may be false, or may be imagined. Nevertheless it deals with sensitive matters in the lives of others.

At stake is the future of a dozen or so other people. The gossip will affect the spouses, children, relatives, and employees. Indeed the whole company may be affected. What started out as an intimate conversation between two friends has taken on the characteristics of a full-blown scandal.

If the president were forced to resign or leave the company, the future prospects for the company's success could be jeopardized. The spouses involved face the prospect of separation or divorce. The children suffer from a broken home and the dissipated income that results from divorce. There is no end to the misery that can ensue. But what about those that persist in gossiping? What happens to them? They remain relatively unscathed. Most likely, they don't even feel any guilt. They feel detached from the whole matter. Perhaps they deal with it in a manner similar to the way two soldiers might deal with a combat situation wherein one gets shot and the other lives. The one that lives feels sorry for the one that got killed, yet inside he feels relieved that it was his buddy that got it and not him. The same is true with gossip. It gives one vicarious pleasure to hear about another's troubles or problems, and as much as one may feel sorry for that person, deep down inside one feels good that it is not happening to oneself.

## From a Management Viewpoint

It is quite true that the more things change, the more they stay the same, and the only things new in the world are the things we haven't read. In the case of gossip and abuses of the tongue, the practice has kept up with the times and has spread with rapidity throughout the modern business organization. It has become a problem that has attracted a lot of executive attention. So much, in fact, that Mr. Harry Gray, when he was the chairman of United Technologies, a leading national defense contractor, saw fit to run a full page ad in the *Wall Street Journal*. The ad read:

### THE SNAKE THAT POISONS EVERYBODY

It topples governments, wrecks marriages, ruins careers, bursts reputations, causes heartaches, nightmares, indigestion, spawns suspicion, generates grief, dispatches innocent people to cry in their pillows. Even its name hisses. Its called gossip. Office gossip. Party gossip. It makes headlines and headaches. Before you repeat a story ask yourself: Is it true? Is it fair? Is it necessary? If not, shut up.

© United Technologies Corporation, March 1981

The ad was part of a series of messages from Mr. Gray to the business world via the *Wall Street Journal*. If the chairman of the board of one of the world's largest corporations believed that gossip was a problem of such significant importance in human relations that he placed an expensive full-page ad to send a message to readers rather

133

than hype a product, there must be genuine concern on the part of America's business leaders.

Organizational gossip is a vivid subspecies of personal conversation. The force of gossip in groups such as those found in a business environment has a double aspect. On one hand the process of the talk itself demonstrates the vitality, intimacy, and attentiveness of the group. As such, it can prove to be a significant force in management as well as organizational culture. On the other hand, the talk itself can have long-term detrimental results.

We have pointed out that gossip is universally recognized as being bad. Yet we know that people persist in indulging in it. So what do we do to steel ourselves against the temptation to jump in and join the crowd? Obviously humans must like to gossip. Is it a basic part of human nature? Is it a fatal flaw in our character? Let's face it, surely everyone of us has partaken at one time or another and probably enjoyed the participation even if it was at someone else's expense. And what is the content of all this gossip? Just about anything under the sun. No story is ever too trivial to stir up responses and set in motion the weaving backwards and forwards of tales and deeds. Gossip constitutes information that takes on a semblance of truth. Whether or not it is accepted as truth depends on the listener.

## Sorting It All Out

The listener who accumulates gossip in sufficient quantities to establish it as fact is able to interpret the gossip and render it as either false or true. The mystery of gossip is inextricably tied to the mysterious human need to talk. Even though we oftentimes say nothing of significance, we still continue to talk even though there is a lack of subject matter.

When we understand why man talks so much for the mere sake of talking, we will probably be better equipped to understand why he prefers to speak and hear evil rather than good. Gossip is a mystery. The mystery is that it can be associated with myth, tradition, and nostalgia. As such it helps people make sense of the present in relation to the past.

If you gather together enough gossip, it becomes information. Enough information in turn can reveal the truth. The power to convert it lies with whoever accumulates the facts, takes command of them, and sorts them out. In this way, you can make gossip work to your advantage without actively participating in it. Listen and accumulate information. Keep your mouth shut and do not volunteer anything. Your role is to hear all and tell nothing. When you have enough pieces, they will fall into place and you will have the whole story.

An example of this is found in the tried and proven methods that detectives use in conducting an investigation. By talking to a lot of individuals, they pick up a lot of gossip, rumors, hearsay, all intertwined together. The detective uses that information to construct a retrospective analysis. After accumulating the information, the detective is able to fit it together to render a conclusion. Because of the fact that just about everything is talked about, most information comes out sooner or later in the form of the spoken word. Human nature's one universal constant is that people love to talk, love to gossip, and they love to generate interpretations of what they hear.

You should cast yourself in the same mold as the detective. Do not participate in the discussions. Simply gather the information, sort it out, and use it to your own advantage.

# Chapter Six

# How to Treat Confidential and Proprietary Information

During World War II, security posters in defense plants read, "Loose lips sink ships." A thousand years ago the Chinese maintained that the only way that a secret could be kept between two people was if one of them were dead. Attempts to control the flow of information from one human to another have met with limited success. Regardless of how strict or how complex the security system is, the information still gets out. Most of the information is never capitalized on. It dissipates. Other information is put to use, often with devastating implications for the party involved. Much of the information is deliberately stolen. In this chapter we will focus on the problems and opportunities that are found in the loose or careless treatment of confidential and proprietary information in business, government, and industry.

## Information Thieves

Information thieves are now rated as corporate enemy number one. U.S. companies are constantly under attack by modern pirates who inflict tens of millions of dollars worth of damage annually in wasted research and development and missed sales. The trade-secret pirates have the upper hand because the laws are weak and outdated. No company would willingly disclose valuable trade secrets, customer lists, or patents to a competitor. Yet many companies expose themselves to precisely those risks by failing to protect themselves against their own employees. Their employees, because of the demands of the job, must have access to the company's vital information. This has created a security problem of significant size and complexity.

In the recent past, the main focus for security and the protection of company property was the area of hard assets. Companies were concerned about theft of property, raw materials, tools, and finished products. The dramatic growth in technology has shifted the emphasis, and ideas and information are now the key elements. Information is now the critical asset in the success of business. This is particularly true in high-technology enterprises where millions of dollars are poured into research and development. New ideas drive an ever-new and constantly evolving technology. Confidentiality of concepts and processes is critical in order to stay ahead of the competition.

Hard assets were relatively easy to protect. Intangibles are extremely difficult to protect. Concepts, ideas, and processes that are embedded in an employee's mind are uncontrollable. It's quite a bit different from searching a lunch box for company property. You can't touch or see what's going out the gate in the brains of your employees.

The large size of an industry *such as the electronic industry* makes it even more difficult to protect a company's assets. As companies multiply, the competition increases. With competition, the pressure intensifies as companies scramble to find new customers and qualified employees. The whole area of employment within a given industry opens up the floodgates for the transfer of information. Employees tend to stay in the same industry. That is where their value lies. That is where they can make the most money. When an employee moves from one company to another within the same industry, the information from the former employer goes with him. This causes employees to disclose proprietary information to the competition or use the information to their own benefit.

Employees are more mobile than they used to be. They change jobs more frequently and tend to stay in the same career field, due to the high levels of specialization that the marketplace requires. As a result of these frequent moves, employees are less likely to be loyal to any one company. They couldn't care less about past allegiances. Their attitude is more one of "What can my next employer do for me that my past employer neglected to do?" or "So what, they owe me."

Added to these factors is still another problem. The current social environment and liberal moral climate has created new outlets for the misuse or theft of property. Drug and alcohol abuse, along with the many social pressures, has caused new temptations for employees. At the same time, the trend throughout the nation is one wherein it is becoming increasingly difficult to do anything about the problem.

Employees are becoming more sensitive to human rights in general and, specifically, to the rights of the individual. As a result they are becoming increasingly litigious and are raising serious questions in the courts about how far a company can go to safeguard its information and other assets.

As a result of all these factors, the theft-of-information and misappropriation cases have increased fourfold in the past ten years, to more than two hundred a year in the United States courts. And that is only the tip of the iceberg. It is estimated that the actual occurrence of these problems is at least ten times that number, as big business often prefers to keep this area private. The surge of information crimes is directly attributable to the increasing value of information.

In a technological world, trade secrets—e.g., formulas, designs, customer lists, plans—are the new gold to be mined in the marketplace. The legal system has not caught up to this development. The laws are weak, inconsistent, and outdated. This gives the thieves a distinct advantage that many have learned to play for all its worth.

The courts are slow to punish the few who are caught

and the penalties are usually light. Only a dozen states have passed the Uniform Trade Secrets Act, and only twenty-five states have enacted new criminal laws that companies need for protection. Where the laws have been enacted, they haven't proved to be of much help. The new laws define "secret" so narrowly that prosecutors have a hard time pursuing thieves that steal such things as customer lists, price lists, or marketing plans. Many companies have come to the conclusion that it is up to the company itself to put the thieves out of business. Even a Federal trade secret law, if enacted, would not solve the problem.

The problem is people. The flow and control of information is an area of human behavior that is exceedingly complex and involved. Ideas slip out through executives, sales people, suppliers, and even cleaning workers. Some peddle the secrets for profit, others because they haven't learned how to manage their mouths. Executives are constantly looking for spies from the outside. The real problem invariably lies on the inside. Disgruntled employees or terminated employees are prime offenders. Many times terminated employees feel that they "own" the information they had a part in compiling. Whole files have disappeared from offices.

In one case a terminated employee set up her computer terminal in her home and used a modem to tap into the company mainframe. She not only gained access to the company's proprietary information, but she used the stolen computer time to work on some of her personal projects—an example of a case of stealing both information and property.

Female spies have extracted state and military secrets from their high-level lovers enticed into the bedroom by devious means. The secrets of the atomic bomb were sold to the Russians. Trade secrets are compromised daily. National defense plans as well as top secret weapon systems are easy prey for anyone that will take the time to wheedle them out from the many sources that are willing to cooperate, either for money or other favors.

Loose lips do indeed sink ships. Sometimes they can sink companies. A case in point is one where a casual remark at a dinner party set off a series of events that cost a company a 50 million dollar contract and a chance at another contract worth almost as much. The way the story goes is that one of the diners, a company vice president, told his dinner companions that he had seen a portion of the competition's bid on a government contract. He then proceeded to tell them that his company would win the contract because their bid was better than the competition's.

Under federal contract procedure, that was a breach of contract procurement regulations and possibly even federal law. The word got out and the vice president's firm was suspended from bidding. Moreover, future contract bids on an additional 50 million dollar contract were also placed in jeopardy. As this company relied heavily on its work for a particular government agency, the future of the firm was placed at risk. You might say that the vice president's loose lips did indeed sink the ship, just as surely as if it had been hit by a torpedo in the North Atlantic.

142

## Silence Is Golden

*Omerta!* In Italy, more specifically in Sicily, the criminal society, commonly known as the Mafia or the Cosa Nostra—and in America, where it is known as "the mob"—has, as one of its key codes of behavior, a code that deals with managing the mouth. It is the Mafia code of silence, and it is called *omerta.* Practically everything the Mafia is involved in is illegal. It is constantly under attack by law enforcement agencies and competing criminal elements. Despite all this, it has managed to survive and indeed may be growing in influence and power.

Aside from brute force, what do you think is the key ingredient of the Mafia's success? You guessed it! They learned long ago not only how to manage their mouths but to silence the mouths of others. Thus, long ago they recognized the *importance* of managing the mouth. In their line of business, when someone said something that he shouldn't have, a "no-no," that person was severely dealt with. The code of the Mafia, despite our aversion to it, is indicative of the importance that the control of vital information plays in human events.

The United States military establishment created a code of conduct for its members that stresses the importance of controlling information. It establishes the ground rules for behavior if one is taken prisoner. The familiar name, rank, and serial number are all that a captured military person is allowed to give. The withholding of all other information is mandated by the code of conduct, and violations of the code are subject to court-martial. The military recognizes that information in wartime is vital to the security of military operations. From the medieval torture racks to the oriental custom of placing bamboo splinters under the fingernails to inflict severe pain, military personnel have been tortured in an effort to make them give information to the enemy. Is it any different in business? Aside from the torture, I don't think so.

If you are occupying a cozy spot in a safe harbor, inside the womb of a massive corporation, you probably won't have too much effect one way or the other on that corporation. If, on the other hand, you are a key player in an organization that is constantly on the edge, every bit of information that leaves your lips can affect the company's fortunes, and with them, your future and your fortune. Just as the military are trained to adhere to the code of conduct in order not to give the enemy vital information, and just as the Mafia practices *omerta* to protect their secrets, so should the well-disciplined manager learn to recognize and respect the importance of treating information properly.

## Rumor Mongers

We have discussed the fact that the psychological underpinnings of humans are such that we love to spread information. There are specific categories of people that deal in giving out or passing on information as a way of life. Chief among those is the rumor monger. There is a breed of cat that thrives on being the first kid on the block with the hottest rumor. It's almost as if that person existed solely for the purpose of priming the grapevine. "Hey, did you hear that so-and-so is getting divorced?" In the announcement to the world at large there is not one shred of compassion for the parties involved. The individual doesn't even know if the statement is true. Rather, the hot scoop syndrome takes over and the rumor monger has to be the first with the "news." He or she is best described as a troublemaker. The way that he or she deals with information, or lack of information, is ridiculous. The rumor monger gets others' attention by actively seeking out hot news. In a manner similar to selling newspaper extras, the rumor monger "sells" his information to his acquaintances for the price of gaining their attention for a brief period of time. The rumor monger then enjoys a moment of bliss as the center of attraction. Most of the time, others will listen to what this person has to say. After a while, however, they will make certain that they don't tell that character anything, for fear that he will broadcast it to the world.

## How to Deal with Rumors

Is there any such thing as a groundless rumor? People are not stupid. They do not make things up and spread make believe around. Rather they take a piece of information and spread it around. As the information is passed from one person to the next, it gets changed around. It can be embellished, exaggerated, stretched, altered—whatever it takes to make it interesting to the next person in the chain. Yet underlying the rumor is a grain of truth. Without that grain, the rumor would quickly die out. The old maxim to "take everything with a grain of salt" means that you assume it is true but you reserve the option to believe it is partly false. With a rumor, you should believe that there is some basis, or actual truth, in the rumor or it would not persist in spreading.

Quite frequently the same rumor may come to you from separate directions. It is highly improbable that two sources could fabricate the same falsehood simultaneously. Somewhere, somehow, somebody gave cause for the rumor. What do you do about it? You can check it out. Call the butt of the rumor up and find out the true story, if any. Is this risky? Yes, it is. But if the rumor is serious enough and it impacts you or your business associates, then you should get it out into the open so that it can be dealt with before irrevocable harm is done.

## Look Out For Moles

There is a leak in this organization! How many times have you heard that exclamation. Invariably it is true. There is a leak in the organization. The most widespread cause of leaks is so-called moles. The term "mole" gained popularity during the Watergate scandal in the early seventies. Since then the term has been used to describe any source of information *within* an organization.

A perfect example of this is a case wherein a high-level executive was terminated from his position. His faithful secretary was promoted to become executive secretary to the division president. The fired executive began to create a new business that would be in direct competition with his former company. He needed information on what the management team at his former company was planning in the way of competing programs. His former secretary, who handled all the correspondence for her boss, had access to all the confidential memos that her boss was copied in on. She simply made copies of all the pertinent memos and mailed them to her former boss and, now, close personal friend. Needless to say, the ex-employee then had the same information as the president of the corporation. He used the information to launch a competing business.

## Watch Out For the Hot Scoop Syndrome

There is another type of person that thrives on dispensing hot news. He or she scoops everyone. "Hey, did you hear that Al got fired?" Nowhere is there a shred of compassion for the party involved. Rather, the hot scoop idiot must spread the news as fast as he or she can. Here again, being in the limelight or in the know is what drives these people. They get satisfaction by finding out things ahead of everyone else and then letting everyone else know that they knew it first. For some weird reason the hot scoop artist almost feels proprietary about the news: "Remember, you heard it from me first, and if you don't believe me, check it out yourself." After a while this turns people off.

147

## Be Able to Recognize the Inner Circle

Within every organization there is an inner circle. It is called by various names, e.g., the team, the clique, the cadre, the "ins," and so on. These are the people that are the key players in the company. They run the company. They make the major decisions, they guide and direct the operation, and they set the goals and execute the plans that make or break the company or the organization. These are the doers. The exchange of information within the inner circle is about as open as it could be anywhere.

There are no secrets among this group. To the outside world, however, just about everything that transpires in this group is secret. In days of old, the knights of the Round Table gathered for a meeting. A rose was placed above the table. Everything that was discussed from that point on, under the rose, or "sub-rosa," was secret. It was the knights' duty to keep it a secret. The same is true nowadays.

## Guard Against the Blabbermouths

"Sorry, I simply couldn't contain myself." It's the blabbermouth! There is a breed of corporate animal that doesn't give a hoot about the company's private information. These people blab everything. They have a total irreverence for everything and treat sensitive information as if it were a joke. These individuals know only one loyalty and that is to themselves. They care nothing about the company they work for; they only care about the short-term rewards that the company can provide them. Usually

148

they only stay with a company for a short period of time, until they either get fired or quit because they "do not fit in" with the company culture. Which really means, "Just because I speak up and tell a few stories out of school, the management around here doesn't like me or trust me."

## Naive or Just Plain Stupid?

Call them stupid, call them inexperienced, or call them naive. They are the ones that always spill the beans. "Gee, I'm not sure, I may have mentioned it to my girl friend, but I never thought it would get back to Mr. Smith. How was I to know that she was his sister-in-law?"

It must have been a shock to Mr. Smith to find out that he was getting fired. Especially hearing it from his sister-in-law. I wish I had never seen that letter of termination.

## Honest Sinners (of Commission and Omission)

Quite often you may be caught in a situation wherein you transmit information to a third party without any intention of doing so. Perhaps you provide a small but vital piece of information that seems innocuous on the surface yet, when put in context with the rest of the pieces that the listener has, becomes a key piece in the mosaic. Hence, unwittingly, you play a key role in the process and become a source of information.

Sometimes it's what you don't say that counts. The expression on your face is all it takes to either affirm or deny the truth. Very few of us can maintain an unreadable expression. When confronted with a situation where you are asked to respond to something, it is very difficult to skirt the issue by remaining silent. Your body language—the expression on your face, the look in your eyes, the position of your brow, and all your other body movements—add up to a transmission of your answer without you saying a single word. The blush on your face can provide the answer, or the easily read look of total disbelief or bewilderment can confirm or deny a statement. You don't have to say the words out loud. Your body actions can give you away.

The whole purpose of the lie detector test is to measure the body reactions that occur when a person is confronted with questions. The average, honest person's body signs will change when he or she tells a lie. The telling of a lie goes against the person's basically honest behavior pattern, and the difficulty they encounter, when forced to tell a lie, can be recorded.

If, on the other hand, the person is a habitual liar and no emotion is expressed when he or she is forced to lie, then the machine won't record any change, because the lying behavior pattern is "normal" for that person, hence there is no physical difference that can be measured.

## Third Parties (Crisscross Your Heart and Hope to Die)

"Psst! Want to hear a good one?"

"Yeah!"

"Promise me you won't tell a soul?"

"Okay, okay, I promise."

"Swear on your mother's grave?"

"Okay, I swear on my mother's grave. Furthermore may my father die of chicken pox if I tell anyone."

Information is passed from one person to another with the basic premise that the person receiving the information can be trusted with it. The question, in reality, comes down to this: Is absolute trust really possible? The answer is that it is not. At least, not in its purest form. Information, no matter how important it is to any individual, under any circumstances, when passed on to a third party not directly concerned with the issues or problems, tends to become diluted, colored, or trivialized.

Values are blurred and the receiver does not feel any degree of responsibility for safeguarding the information entrusted to him or her. Further, if the till is involved, i.e., money or the bottom line, then the information will be put to whatever use the possessor deems necessary to further his or her own objectives.

The advanced state of technology drives the speed at which information can be transmitted, and it also drives the need to accumulate information on computers, tape recorders, and the like. In the past it required elaborate note taking, recording, and filing to store and retrieve information. Now it is simply a matter of keying it into the computer memory bank, putting it on tape or disc, or using the video camera to accurately record information.

Perception has, in effect, become reality. So much information is available and so many subjects are dealt with in a single business day that the perception of them becomes the reality. Oftentimes the perception is a distortion of the truth.

## Relatives, Best Friends, and Trusted Confidants

As we pointed out earlier, it is very difficult to keep things to oneself. Basic human nature compels people to open up and discuss what is on their minds. Quite often they need to discuss things with people that are not directly involved in the problem. They could be relatives, a best friend, or other confidant. The tendency to bare one's soul and get things off one's chest is overwhelming, and quite often individuals will relate highly detailed information to third parties that have absolutely no interest in the subject. What they do not realize is that once the information is told to a third party, it will invariably spread to other parties and eventually will end up in the lap of someone that does have a vested interest. When that occurs, the information takes on new meaning and significance and can directly impact the problem.

## Paraphrasing Doesn't Always Work

Paraphrasing is a method whereby confidential information can be discussed by rephrasing the essential content to hide the true meaning of the subject matter. By choosing words and phrases carefully, the heart of the subject can be disguised so that the listener who is not privy to the specifics will not be able to figure out what is being discussed. But who is kidding whom? It is so difficult to paraphrase, to pick and choose words that are seemingly unrelated to the specific plan or program, that any person with half a brain can put two and two together and figure out what is going on. Furthermore, if the individual has a shred of information on the same subject, gained from another source, it becomes very easy to decipher.

Individuals who believe that paraphrasing is a safeguard that allows them to discuss sensitive subjects out in the open are mistaken. The only foolproof way to discuss secret information is to ensure that there are no third parties listening.

## Don't Loosen Up Your Tongue with Booze

Earlier, as you may recall, we touched on the power of alcohol to loosen up the tongue. It's a fact, alcohol will do it every time. *In vino veritas* is an ancient Latin expression that means in wine there is truth. Oftentimes the most highly disciplined individual, who wouldn't even tell his or her mother a secret, will open up to a complete stranger after a drink or two. Liquor lowers inhibitions. Individuals that normally exercise good control over their behavior will open up under the influence of booze and will discuss many subjects that they would not even hint at were they sober. In most cases, on the morning after, they regret it.

The tendency to open up and reveal your inner self while under the influence of liquor can be controlled. First of all you should realize that no one is perfect. People say weird things while under the influence. However, by recognizing that small failures can lead to success, you can develop better self-control. Recognizing and admitting your failures is the first step to future success. Over time, trial and error will help you develop control. You will be better equipped to deal with the problem by understanding the degree of influence that liquor is having on you. You will know how many drinks it takes before you start to get "loose," and you will regulate your intake accordingly. The important thing is to know your limit—gain insight into your own shortcomings in this very sensitive area and behave accordingly. The way you handle your drinking, and the way you manage your mouth when under the influence, can have a tremendous effect on your professional career and your personal life.

## Avoid the Trap of Vicarious Pleasure

People love to tell tales out of school. They derive pleasure from it. If the story has to do with someone else's problems or troubles, all the better. As long as it does not affect us personally, we seem to enjoy openly discussing others' woes. People actually take delight and gain pleasure in such discussions. A legendary American hero is the strong, silent type. This rare individual is physically strong and mentally tough. The fact that he or she is silent is very revealing. It tells us that silence is considered to be a virtue. This individual does not indulge in sins of the mouth. He or she does not spread rumors or participate in gossip, and never, never speaks ill of another human. Unfortunately, this silver-screen image is just that, a silver-screen image. In reality this person does not exist. Every human, at one time or another, falls into the trap of committing what I call misuse of the mouth. It is part of being human. It is a human frailty, but people even take pleasure in it. It is highly evident and is with us all the time. If you recognize it for what it is, then you can guard against the temptation to participate.

## Don't Build Yourself Any Maginot Lines

After World War I the French were once again filled with the fear of being invaded from the east. With potential enemies, such as the Germans, rebuilding their armed forces, the French conceived and built an elaborate wall that extended for hundreds of miles along the border of France. The wall was supposed to provide protection. It was heavily fortified and defended. It was called the Maginot Line. It was intended to keep the enemy at bay if France was invaded, and many felt that it would solve the problem, once and for all, of having enemy armies invade France from the east. At the beginning of World War II the Germans simply went around the wall and invaded France anyway. The wall did not accomplish very much toward protecting France from invasion.

Individuals establish their own, personal, Maginot Lines. They build defense mechanisms that they feel will help them overcome problems encountered in safeguarding information. Organizations in business and government do the same thing. They establish elaborate security measures. They classify documents, keep track of them, conduct background investigations on people in order to provide them with access clearances. They utilize safes, guards, ID cards, surveillance equipment, and all sorts of physical safeguards. Individuals are trained to ferret out potential leaks. They use psychological tests to uncover and detect individual weaknesses. They delve into the motives behind individual behavior in order to understand what kind of information certain individuals can be trusted with. Despite all these safeguards and regardless of what security measures are taken, information gets out and falls into the wrong hands.

## Look Out For All Ears

Every organization has one. That busy individual who goes all-out to gather information. This individual doesn't miss a trick. He or she must be "in the know." People like this cannot stand being shunted aside and having information withheld from them. As a result, they relentlessly "pump" others for information.

"Hey, Charlie, what's going on in the front office? The boss looks like he's under tremendous pressure lately. Is there any truth to the rumor that we lost a major account? What's with his secretary Linda? She looks like death warmed over. What the hell is going on? Clue me in."

What Charlie doesn't know is that his friend has asked three or four other people in the office the same question. His friend is one of the busybodies that occupy themselves by picking up information in bits and pieces until the mosaic takes form. Once the pieces are together, then the real fun begins. The "all ears" turns into "all mouth." If the busybodies can pick up enough dirt by making the rounds, then they can "dish the dirt" later on.

The reason they do this is simple. Their primary motive is to make themselves feel important. Their secondary motive is to get someone to listen to them and thus gain the center ring of attention for a brief period of time. Interestingly enough, they never seem able to create any interest in themselves based on their own accomplishments or their own merits. It is always at the expense of someone else.

## All Your Knowledge Will Be Folly Unless Grace Guides It

Knowledge is folly unless it is used wisely and prudently. Knowledge in its purest sense is power. If you are in the know, and you understand all aspects of a given situation, then chances are you can wield a great deal of power. The only people that can challenge your power are those that know more about the subject than you do. There is a story going around about a very powerful corporate executive who would completely stifle any discussion with his subordinates by bellowing out, "Who are you to question me? You do not have all the pieces. Only I have all the pieces, therefore I will make the decisions around here."

Even the most informed subordinates would cower or cave in under this harangue from the boss. After all, if they weren't really sure if they had more or less information than the boss, they had to acquiesce and allow him to exercise autocratic rule over the organization.

## Protecting Inside Information

Inside information, does it have a price tag? Recent Wall Street scandals answered that question when over a billion dollars was rung up in ill-gotten gains as a result of trading stocks on inside information. On a smaller scale this is done every day by corporate managers and other players that are privy to inside information about the business activities of the company they are associated with.

The value of inside information is equal to the value of a crystal ball. After all, why concern yourself with tomorrow's news, when you are creating the news today? Did you ever hear of a corporate executive losing money on an inside trade. Wouldn't it be a unusual to pick up the *Wall Street Journal* and read about a case wherein a corporate executive was being investigated because of making a trade that he lost money on. Don't bet on it. The only time a corporate executive would lose money on an insider trade would be if an external event took place about which he or she had no prior knowledge and hence no control over.

## Putting the Pieces Together to Create Something of Value

In the business world it is quite often the case that seemingly small bits of information can be worth their weight in gold. A major corporation with headquarters in New York

City justified an executive dining room to its stockholders on the basis of providing a controlled dining area where executives could dine with business associates without being seen by all kinds of outsiders. The company was in the entertainment business, and all it takes to smell a deal being put together in that business is to see two key people talking to each other. The astute observer can put two and two together with ease and come up with an answer. A piece of information here, a piece of information there, and pretty soon the big picture starts to come into focus.

During the inside-trading scandal that rocked the financial world in the late eighties, the arbitrageurs actually hired private detectives to stake out office buildings to see if they could spot the comings and goings of certain key people who were working on acquisitions and mergers. The comings and goings, combined with leaks and intentional misconduct consisting of passing out critical inside information, resulted in millions of dollars trading hands and huge illegal profits being made at the expense of other innocent bystander stockholders.

Fortunately for those people, and the rest of us, the culprits were found out. The story does not end there, however. It continues. Wherever there is money to be made, the bits and pieces of information that are needed to figure out financial deals are carefully and methodically gathered up. Sometimes the information is obtained legally and sometimes it is obtained illegally, by eavesdropping, wiretapping, and intercepting mail and messages. All the sophisticated techniques formerly confined to the FBI or a James Bond movie are now falling into fairly common use in the big-stake games that are being played in the big-business world. The value of information is directly proportional to the value of the chips on the table. If one knows what cards the other fellow is holding, it certainly reduces the risk. Likewise, if you are aware of the risks involved in handling information, then you should go out of your way to protect and safeguard your knowledge and reduce your risk accordingly.

## Watch Out! You Never Know Who Is Listening

In one ear and out the other is not always the case. Oftentimes it's in one ear and out the mouth for a quick buck. A piece of information about a competitor's problems with its new line could be parlayed into a sale of your competitive product. And vice versa. A few comments in the elevator, a few comments on the plane to a perfect stranger, a comment here or there by one of the accountants, and pretty soon the rumors start to fly. Where did they come from? They came from you and you and you. "Our next generation computer will swamp the competition." "Oh, when is it coming out?" "I don't know. It's supposed to be top secret, but everyone is talking about it. It goes under the code name Centaur."

# Chapter Seven

# Keeping a Secret a Secret

How good are you at safeguarding information, keeping secrets, and making sure that you do not unwittingly divulge information to the wrong party? How good are you at being able to manage and control information that is entrusted to your care? There are many situations you will find yourself thrust into where, for your own good, you will have to conceal information from others, where compromising information can have serious repercussions. Fortunately, there are a number of ploys, distractions, techniques, and other bits of gamesmanship that can be brought to bear on the situation and help you to keep a secret a secret. Here are a few of them.

## Reverse Body Language

Earlier we learned that it is not always what you say that counts, it is how it is interpreted. The slightest nuance, innuendo, or subtlety in your conversation can broadcast the exact meaning of your position more accurately than you would ever imagine. All too often the receiver of the message reads between the lines and gets the message regardless of what words are being used. An arched brow, a twinkle in the eye, a loose metaphor, or a frown can tell the message-receiver far more than a noun, verb, or adjective. This is not to say that your delivery must be deadpan, but that the use of animation or any other embellishment goes a long way toward revealing your true thoughts and ideas. As we now know, the use of body language is great when you want people to get the message. The opposite is true when you want to conceal or hide information. The worse you are at communicating, the better off you are in terms of keeping the listener in the dark.

## Shrug Your Shoulders and Employ Negative Nonverbals

Negative nonverbals can get you off the hook in a situation where speaking can get you into hot water. For example, you are in a meeting and a colleague is making a statement to the chairman. The colleague turns to you and says, "Isn't that right, Joe?" You have all the facts, however you do not wish to respond to that question for several reasons. One reason may be that it will appear that you are supporting your colleague's position. Another may be that you will be giving away the fact that you have knowledge of the situation, and that knowledge is privileged. So what do you do? You shrug your shoulders. You put body language to use, however in this case it is for negative reinforcement. But what does that mean? It could mean several things. It could mean that you are indifferent. It could mean that you don't know the answer. It could mean that you don't care. The beauty part of a negative nonverbal is that it is open to various interpretations. Shoulder shrugging, rolling the eyes, making faces, body gestures, a frown, a smile, and so on, are all open to interpretation the same way that the *Mona Lisa*'s smile is open to interpretation. What this buys for you is the ability to respond to questions without revealing your true feelings.

## Be Smart and Play Dumb

A useful tool that can be used to retain information is to simply play dumb, like the three monkeys that see no evil, hear no evil, and speak no evil. You mimic the speechless one. When someone broaches a delicate subject, you simply act as if you know nothing about it. No matter how much information you have in the way of facts and figures, you simply deny any knowledge of the situation. This can be accomplished by playing dumb. All you have to do is say as little as possible and act naive at the same time. This can be accomplished by engaging the other person with simple questions. The questions should indicate that the information the person is seeking is totally foreign or new to you. Further, you haven't the slightest idea what the person is driving at. Any clues that the other person gives you to the subject matter at hand should be treated as new revelations to you and things that you know nothing about. You can exclaim, "Oh, is that a fact?" or "What's the scoop?" or "Gosh, what could have caused that?" or "Golly, that's the first I've heard of that situation."

You act out the role of having little or no knowledge of the situation. You play the role of a highly receptive listener, and you do not contribute any valuable information to the conversation. Your role is passive and you simply listen. You act as though you are hearing about the subject for the first time and know nothing about it. Outwardly, you act as though you are totally unaware of anything that your colleague is revealing to you, either by his or her statements or by the line of questions being asked. To take it to extremes, you exhibit little, if any, interest in what he or she is telling you and you conceal your emotions.

## Go Off on a Tangent

In a situation where you are in possession of sensitive information and you are confronted by an individual that tries to pin you down, simply go off on tangents. Do this enough and you will discourage any further inquiries. This can be accomplished by avoiding giving any direct answers to questions while at the same time introducing totally different subjects. By taking the individual "off on a tangent," or as they say on the farm, "around the barn," you can avoid answering questions. For example, assume that you know that your boss has just resigned and one of your colleagues asks you point-blank if that is true. You know for a fact that it is true. You just heard it directly from your boss not less than ten minutes ago. Rather than answer the question with a direct "yes" or "no," you shrug your shoulders and say, "I don't know if that's true or not, but I know for a fact that the company is thinking of merging with XYZ company. I heard just recently that serious discussions were taking place, what do you think of that?" If your colleague persists in asking about your manager, you persist in talking about the planned merger. The person will soon get the message and will stop asking you about your boss. Going off on tangents can be very effective in avoiding answers to questions.

## Change the Subject

If you don't like the line of questions and you don't want to answer them any further, change the subject. It's easy to do. It's called "shifting gears." You start out by answering questions that your colleagues are asking, but prior to getting into the crux of the subject you "shift gears" and change the subject. This can be accomplished by talking fast, covering a lot of territory, and changing the subject several times without giving your colleague a chance to get a question in edgewise. Only the most experienced adversary will re-introduce the original question. To do so, he or she must run the risk of coming across as an interrogator. Once that happens, you can quickly gain the upper hand and close down the whole conversation. No one has to answer questions "when they are asked in that tone of voice . . ." Shifting gears is very effective in getting away from any subject that you do not wish to discuss.

## Deception Versus Lying

There is a tremendous difference between deceiving and lying. From a professional point of view a deception is carried out to protect information from those with no legitimate reason to have access to it. Lying, on the other hand, is a compromise of integrity. It should be avoided. To elaborate on the distinction: deception is carried out when a group of individuals conspire to ensure that the sanctity of their mission is protected. A liar generally acts as a lone individual and his or her lies are self-serving with an illegal or immoral intent. Quite frequently in government and industry it is a perfectly normal and accepted practice to carry out deception. The intent of a deception is to keep the enemy or adversary in the dark to protect and safeguard vital information. It is a common practice that is exercised at the highest levels of the federal government and the highest levels in the private sector.

## Pulling in the Reins

A simple but effective practice in controlling the flow of information is by direct action. You can pull in the reins and turn the conversation around by being blunt and to the point. You can say, "I don't mean to be rude, but you are off base. That subject should not be talked about in public." Or you can say, "I will tell you here and now, right to your face, that you are treading on thin ice by repeating that information. Cut it out!" Or you can say, "I beg your pardon, but around here we do not take these matters lightly, and the information that you are openly discussing is better left unsaid."

The technique of pulling in the reins is tough to use if you are not a strong person. When used, however, it gets results! Of that you can be sure. Many a conversation has been stopped dead in its tracks by this technique, and quite often the offending party has sheepishly acquiesced.

## Drag in a Red Herring or Two

One way of avoiding having to answer delicate questions or otherwise be placed in a position where you may be forced to divulge sensitive or protected information is to drag in a red herring. This expression means simply that you introduce or drag into the conversation a different subject from the one under discussion.

For example, assume that you are being questioned by a subordinate as to the amount of pay that another employee is earning. The subordinate feels that he is underpaid, that the other employee is being paid more than he is, and he is trying to find out the amount. You know that if that information is revealed you will have a serious morale problem on your hands. Rather than answer the question, you drag in a red herring. You can drag in as many other issues or red herrings as it takes to avoid answering his question directly. Here are some examples: "Charlie, how much was your last increase?" "Charlie, how do you feel about your salary progression to date?" "Charlie, do you feel that you are being paid fairly compared to the marketplace for your skills and experience?" "Charlie, what do you see as your next step in this organization? Where do you want to be down the road two or three years from now?"

## Throw the Dogs Off the Scent

An effective method of protecting sensitive information is to skirt the subject. This will result in not having to address the subject head-on. This is easier to do than one might expect—people are very reluctant to bore in with their questions. They will frequently ask "surface" questions and avoid the heart of the matter.

I was involved in a training session that had to do with questioning techniques. We were steeped in the concept of "asking the fourth question." The "fourth question" is the one that elicits a definitive answer. One or two questions is very seldom adequate to get to a satisfactory level of understanding. The concept of the fourth question was simply to ask enough questions to gain the information you need.

Because people are prone to back off and not ask the "fourth question," you have ample opportunity to be vague and evasive in your answer. Very few people will take you to task and continue to bore away. As a result, you can skirt the issue without having to reveal anything that you don't want to reveal.

You can accomplish this in two steps. First, provide the questioner with a very shallow answer. Make it appear that you know very little about the subject under discussion. Save some information for the second question. When you are asked the second question, you throw out another teensy bit of information, and pretend that that is about all you know about the subject. Chances are the questioner will stop asking questions at that point. Usually the questions will stop because the questioner is not very aggressive, or does not want to appear rude or overbearing. The conversation may go something like this:

"Say John, what's the scoop on that new software package that you guys are working on?"

"I don't know too much about it."

"Well I understand that you are heavily involved in it. What is the schedule for completing it?"

"Not really, I've only got a minor part in it."

If the questioner does ask a third question, then you simply respond with a minimum of information, which you give out while acting as if bored by the conversation. Very rarely will the questioner continue to try to get you to open up. Invariably, he or she will back off and the "fourth question" will never be asked. In turn, the questioner will never understand what you do or do not know.

## Deny It Outright

Outright denial of the information is sometimes called for. If the other, friendly techniques fail, then you have no alternative but to deny, deny, deny. I use the expression "friendly techniques" to describe a situation wherein the conversation is amiable and no one gets his nose out of joint. If the questioner relentlessly bores in, your only recourse is to deny outright any and all knowledge of the subject. For example, if you cannot throw your questioner off the scent by changing the subject, and he or she resorts to cross-examining you with question after question to the point where you feel you are being interrogated, then you have no alternative other than to shut the conversation down. This can be done effectively by saying, "I'm sorry, but I must be on my way" or "I'm sorry, but that is classified information" or, plainly and simply, "I can't say, one way or the other."

Having to avoid telling a friend something you know is unpleasant. The facts of life are such, however, that you are caught between a rock and a hard place. If you tell, you will compromise the trust that was placed in you when you were provided with sensitive information. If you don't tell, you run the risk of alienating a friend. A lot depends on the culture in the organization.

In the federal government and in the military, everyone goes around saying, "I'm sorry, but that's classified information and you do not have a need to know." This latter statement stems from the national security program, which is based on the concept of containing and confining information to only those individuals that have an actual reason to have the information. In other words, only those individuals that must have the information in order to carry out their responsibilities are allowed access to the information. Providing, of course, that they have the proper security clearance.

In a situation like that, the lesser of the two evils is shutting down the conversation and risking alienating your colleague. Chances are that your colleague will, in the long run, respect you more for your strength in controlling sensitive information. On occasion you will run into a situation where the opposite will be true. A relationship may go down the drain as a result of your not being open and telling all to certain individuals. For your own piece of mind, you must be true to yourself and respect the trust that was placed in you, regardless of whose nose gets out of joint. Stick to your guns and let the chips fall where they may. Clearly, if you want to protect the information at any cost, then you must be prepared to take the heat.

## Set Up a Deniability Scenario

The management of information has become very sophisticated. It is a common practice to plan ahead for contingencies to ensure that high-level managers can retain their credibility. An example of this type of contingency planning has to do with the concept of deniability. Here is how it works. Assume that a high-level manager feels very strongly about a subject. The subject is introduced at a board of directors' meeting and it gets shot down. The top-level manager feels that he is right and the board is wrong. He wants to pursue his plan of action. If he does it directly and he is found out, the board will fire him. What can he do? He enlists a loyal staff member—a tried and true employee who understands exactly what he wants. The staff member puts the plan into action and does not tell his boss what he is doing. Not one shred of information is ever passed from him to the boss. In the event that the board of directors finds out about the project, the boss can deny all knowledge of it.

The scheme was set up to ensure that the boss would be able to honestly deny any involvement. The staff member, of course, would take the rap for the project, knowing full well that he would be well taken care of off-line. The risk may be worth taking. If the project is successful, popular support among the stockholders will overcome any pressure from the board. If the project fails or is discovered by the board, then a "scapegoat" is already in place. In either case the top-level manager is "safe".

The tactic of deniability, although not the most positive way to do business, is used more and more to provide a protective shield for top-level managers. Its use is driven by issues that are increasingly subjected to diverse political, social, and environmental concerns.

## Feign Total Disbelief

An effective method of avoiding having to divulge sensitive information is to feign disbelief. This is done by making declarations and by asking questions. You never answer any question, because to do so will put you in a position where you could not escape except by lying, and above all you don't ever want to lie. And you won't have to. By using the various techniques available to you, you can exasperate your questioner without ever having to resort to lying. To feign disbelief, you make the questioner believe that you are hearing the information for the first time and that you do not believe it. For example, a colleague approaches you and says, "Say, Joe, I understand that you cracked the XYZ account."

The fact of the matter is you have presented your proposal to the XYZ company and they have assured that you will be awarded the contract. However, several conditions must be met and you are not sure that your firm is willing to meet them. If the word gets out that you are that close to the contract, and the street hears about it, then the whole project may be jeopardized. You must not let any information leak out. You consider the various techniques that you can use to stifle the subject and you decide to feign total disbelief. To feign total disbelief, you utilize questions and exclamations. In this case your response might be "Are you serious? What are you talking about?"

Your colleague tells you what he or she is talking about and you exclaim, "No way!" or "That's ridiculous!"

You disclaim everything that your colleague broaches, and you create the impression that everything that is being said is absurd, untrue, and totally unbelievable. You convince him or her that it is all news to you and furthermore you do not believe any of it. You do not ask any questions because if you do you run the risk of prolonging the conversation. Your goal is to shut down the conversation as fast as you can and leave the impression that you know nothing of the situation and, even if the situation could possibly exist, you simply do not do not believe it.

## Conclusion

By now you should have a pretty good idea of all the little bits and pieces required to make you more effective at managing your mouth. The concepts and procedures described in this book have been developed by the author through years of practical experience gained in supervisory, management, and executive positions in both government and industry.

Because few, if any, formal training programs exist on this subject, experience still seems to be the best teacher. Learning by experience, however, is a slow process. Further, many individuals do not learn from experience because they fail to recognize the underlying problem. As a result, it is difficult to learn to manage one's mouth simply as a result of experience.

Left to trial and error, the process takes a long time to show any progress and, in some cases, may never show results. The basic reason is that the process is invisible. It takes place in the mind and does not lend itself to open scrutiny by others. No one can follow you around and point out every little thing that you do wrong. No one can read your mind, or gauge your innermost feelings.

Thus, the primary purpose of this book is to make the process visible to the reader—to point the way for the reader, in short time, to the many considerations involved in managing verbal interaction.

Application of the ideas expressed in this book will not come about automatically. A conscious effort will be required to avoid reverting back to old behaviors. Improvement will come about in direct proportion to the level of motivation and the effort put forth.

Progress can be measured from time to time by reviewing the material contained in this book, by comparing old responses to new ones, and by assessing your current proficiency in verbal interactions. Hopefully we have provided you with a few more arrows for your quiver of personal skills. Now it's up to you to put them to good use. Good luck to you and your mouth!

# INDEX

# Index